Praise for COHERENT STRATEGY AND EXECUTION

"*An easy read with a compelling message. Gets to the heart of organizational challenges and pitfalls leaders face. Leaders at every level in the organization must take stock of the need to transform their business and themselves.*"

LARRY KELLNER
FORMER CHAIRMAN AND CEO
CONTINENTAL AIRLINES

"*As the book unfolds, you find yourself squirming in your seat because you can see the metaphorical train wreck co⌐ ⌐his book allows you to see not only the tools, but experie⌐ ⌐tion in situations that ring true to experienced l⌐*

"*Every serious leader will ⌐ ⌐ding* COHERENT STRATEGY A ⌐ ⌐ou to *rethink your leadership approac⌐*"

KIM D.
CHIEF ADMINISTRATIVE OFFICER
AIR LIQUIDE USA LLC

"COHERENT STRATEGY AND EXECUTION *brings together all the strategic elements of running an enterprise. What makes this book so powerful is that it translates somewhat sterile concepts from traditional strategy textbooks into the richness of the human experience and dialogue so crucial to their understanding and effective implementation. It is a great informative read for both experienced and emerging leaders.*"

LANE SLOAN
FORMER PRESIDENT
SHELL CHEMICAL

"COHERENT STRATEGY AND EXECUTION changed my perspective on leading and running a company. I knew I needed improvements in my organization, and I had tried to solve them myself, but never quite succeeded at the level I knew was possible.

"This book has provided me the context, the baby-steps to crystallize the strategic aspects of my business, and the method to bring it all together. You are doing yourself a disservice by not implementing what is in this book."

BRYANT PRICE
PRESIDENT AND CEO
AGAMA ADVERTISING

"COHERENT STRATEGY AND EXECUTION provides realistic and practical takeaways. How to leverage the right resources in the organization to handle difficult situations? How to develop the right leadership perspective to work with subordinates, peers and superiors? How to manage a team?

"Personally, the most impactful takeaway was the introduction to what the book calls, the recliner exercises. These exercises are now part of my daily routine."

GIRISH HEMRAJANI
VICE PRESIDENT - TREASURER
ION GEOPHYSICAL

"COHERENT STRATEGY AND EXECUTION engaged me in its story so deeply, I experienced the CEO's emotions and felt I was struggling with the issues he faced.

"Having read the book, I am much more sensitive about how I enroll those important to my success into partnership with me. This story provides lots of opportunity for self evaluation."

JOHN O'DELL, DIRECTOR, ALUMNI DEVELOPMENT
C.T. BAUER COLLEGE OF BUSINESS
UNIVERSITY OF HOUSTON
FORMER CEO, EXTREMETIX

"COHERENT STRATEGY AND EXECUTION is particularly well-suited to the classroom setting as a complement to standard texts and articles on strategic management.

"It goes well beyond a typical case study by addressing not only key principles in strategy, but also presenting the people and organizational issues that inevitably complicate the subject."

OSAMA I. MIKHAIL, PhD
PROFESSOR AND DIRECTOR
FLEMING CENTER FOR HEALTHCARE MANAGEMENT
UNIVERSITY OF TEXAS

"Why is that sometimes CEOs with extensive industry background fail, while CEOs from other industries come in and turnaround those failing companies? The answer is certain fundamental management and leadership aspects.

"COHERENT STRATEGY AND EXECUTION seamlessly and succinctly ties together the fundamental aspects for running and growing an organization. No manager can ignore the issues addressed in this parable."

SHARAD BORLE, PhD
ASSOCIATE PROFESSOR OF MARKETING
JESSE H. JONES GRADUATE SCHOOL OF MANAGEMENT
RICE UNIVERSITY

"Most entrepreneurs have powerful ideas and undying passion, but many lack the experience and perspective to successfully manage and grow their companies.

"COHERENT STRATEGY AND EXECUTION is an easy-to-follow resource for helping entrepreneurs understand and appreciate what they are lacking — in management and leadership skills. An absolute must-read and must-follow for achieving business success."

ASHOK RAO
PRESIDENT, THE INDUS ENTREPRENEURS, HOUSTON
CHAPTER; CEO, EXCALIBUR PICTURES

"COHERENT STRATEGY AND EXECUTION takes on the difficult issues facing corporations by realistically depicting the environment and the challenges. This book provides a distillation of the concepts critical for effective strategic planning and execution.

"Every executive should understand and appreciate the concepts in this book to eliminate ambiguity and confusion in their organization. It will help improve focus on the critical drivers for the business, and improve alignment among teams and team members."

SANJAYA SOOD
GLOBAL VICE PRESIDENT
SCHLUMBERGER

"To succeed, entrepreneurs need both creativity and discipline. The business management method offered in COHERENT STRATEGY AND EXECUTION is a valuable tool to help entrepreneurs strike the balance between structure and flexibility. Every entrepreneur must answer the practical questions this book raises."

PAUL FRISON
FOUNDING CEO AND EXECUTIVE VICE CHAIRMAN
HOUSTON TECHNOLOGY CENTER

"COHERENT STRATEGY AND EXECUTION offers valuable, practical insights into developing and executing strategy. Anyone who has had to be a change agent in a company with set ways will benefit from the concepts presented, particularly with respect to the impact required on the organization's culture."

ROBERT PEISER
PRESIDENT, NATIONAL ASSOCIATION OF CORPORATE
DIRECTORS, HOUSTON CHAPTER
CHAIRMAN AND CEO, OMNIFLIGHT

Business is a marathon, not a sprint.

No business can thrive for long without

Clarity and Coherence.

COHERENT
STRATEGY AND EXECUTION

An Eye-opening Parable

about *Transforming Leadership & Management Perspectives*

RAVI GOPALDAS KATHURIA

www.CoherentStrategy.com

Published by SeemaCorp
Copyright © 2010 by Ravi Gopaldas Kathuria
ISBN: 978-0-9821475-0-4
Version: 225 – July 21, 2010

Dedicated to my dear parents,

Gopaldas and Dropadi Kathuria,

to my darling wife,

Seema,

and our loving sons, Amrit and Aayush.

Table of Contents

Introduction

How coherent is your strategy and execution?

Managing and leading an organization is a tremendous challenge. The innumerable business variables, competing agendas, differing expectations, and varied interpretations about what is important in the business create the bedrock for the lack of clarity and coherence, and sub-optimal performance.

What is the situation in your organization? Do executives and employees understand the passion and the purpose behind the organization? Is there ambiguity and/or difference of opinion about the philosophies and the business model? Is strategy the best-kept secret, lost in the day-to-day fire fighting? Is it clear who is accountable for what, and why? Are internal politics preventing the organization from collaborating? Are mega-egos monopolizing the culture?

If your organization and/or your team is experiencing issues similar to those listed above, this business parable is for you and your colleagues.

Successful companies have two common traits — clarity and coherence. They have clarity of purpose, clarity of the business model, clarity of the business direction, and cohesion and coherence among the organization's purpose, philosophies, strategies, work processes, organization design, culture and execution.

Achieving clarity and coherence is easier said than done. It is hard work and it is never-ending work. I have written this book with the single purpose of helping you (whether you are the leader of a big corporation, leader of a small team, or a new entrepreneur) drive clarity and coherence in your thinking and actions.

I present to you a business management method that is succinct and simple, and yet holistic. It has five facets that together cover all the aspects of managing a business. If you understand these five facets, and more importantly, understand their interaction as a system, you will become a better leader and manager, and you will help your organization/team greatly enhance its performance.

Instead of a textbook, I have written this book as a parable to depict a realistic situation, and give you a better sense of the challenges involved. If you are a student, this parable will help you gain a better appreciation for the work environment and the practical skills you need to succeed.

This parable is the story of a CEO, Trent Wertheimer. Trent believes he is perfect and can take his company to the next level. He tries everything he knows, but the harder he tries, the deeper he digs himself into a hole. In this book, you get to understand the eye-opening business transformation of Trent's company, and his painful personal transformation without which success would elude him.

Acknowledgements

When I finished the first version of the book, I was ecstatic. I loved it, I thought it was great. More than fifty versions later, I see now how much the first version needed to improve. It has improved because of the friends, acquaintances, and clients who reviewed the book and gave critical and insightful feedback. I can never sufficiently thank the people who gave their feedback.

Barbara Langham guided me on the right use of the language. She asked the right probing questions that led me to make the book simpler and logical. Lane Sloan, Satin Sanghi, Kim Denney, Trish Winebrenner, Shawn Doherty, Dilip Kathuria, Steve Anderson, Ashish Bhandari, Rohit Chhabra, Bryant Price and Sanjay Sood gave detailed and profound feedback. They challenged me to take the book to the next level. Without their insights, this book wouldn't be where it is today.

I thank Jyoti Gupta for her keen eye, design expertise, and feedback on the book cover.

Osama Mikhail, Paul Frison, Girish Hemrajani, Ashok Rao, Shiv Mathur, Jim Tomforde, Jack Smyth, John O'Dell, Robert Peiser, Walter Ulrich, Sharad Borle, Qusai Maheshri, Hubert Vaz-Nayak, Jayshankar Balan, Anne Davis, Dan Krohn, Arun Pasrija, Trey Shaffer, Mike Schaffner, Troy Greaves, Jeff Linder, Amit Dhawan, Ashok Masand, Keith Frazier, Gary Lassin, Chetan Shah, John Sheptor, Kathy Fourney, Eric Young, Kala Marathi, Corey Prator, Laju Rupani, Murli Rupani, Craig Rickard, Cindy Seffair, Robin

Subramaniam, Chris Cashion, Merri Michaels, Kamal Dama, Anshuma Bhandari, Alok Jain, Jim Compton, Harold Arnold, Dustin Kieschnick and Susan Farrell, all gave feedback on various aspects of the book that helped me improve the book.

The content in this book is inspired from many leading books including:

- *The Discipline of Market Leaders*, Michael Treacy and Fred Wiersema
- *The Goal,* Eliyahu Goldratt, Jeff Cox
- *Competing for the Future*, Gary Hamel and C.K. Prahalad
- *Who Says Elephants Can't Dance,* Louis Gerstner
- *The Balanced Scorecard*, Robert Kaplan and David Norton
- *Execution: The Discipline of Making Things Happen*, Larry Bossidy and Ram Charan

Section 1: Managing Discordantly

Chapter in this section:

Chapter 1: Triumph

Seated at the head of the conference table, Barry Elrod, the CEO of Hintec, led the Monday morning management meeting.

Trent Wertheimer, the VP of sales, seated two seats down from Barry, looked every bit the polished sales professional with his starched white shirt, bright tie, and a precise haircut. He finished providing the sales outlook for the first quarter and then looked at Barry. "To repeat the sales growth we have achieved in the last two years, we must address the issue I have brought up before, our level of customer service."

Barry, a heavier man, dressed more casually, looked down at the table through his glasses and shook his head. "I've heard your complaints." He looked at Hector Jackson, the COO, who also headed customer service and was Barry's right-hand man. "But, Hector gives me a different story."

Trent looked at Hector, who was sitting to the right of Barry. "In the last month alone, at least three customers complained to me they were dissatisfied with the response time and the expertise of our customer support reps."

Hector waved his hand dismissively. "Those are isolated incidents. We have six hundred customers. We can't make them all happy. Ensuring every customer receives perfect service is inordinately expensive," said Hector in his characteristic brusque manner.

Trent looked back at Barry. "These aren't isolated incidents," he refuted. "It's an on-going issue." He looked at Hector with his steely eyes. "My salespeople tell me our customers are refusing to buy more licenses unless we improve our service."

"It's the classic excuse," said Hector with a smirk on his puckered face. "Your salespeople need to improve their selling skills."

Not a big fan of Trent, Maxell Cooley, the VP of marketing, nodded in agreement with Hector's assessment.

Trent felt his blood pressure rise. Barry intervened, "Trent, your team also complains they can't sell because they need more features."

Trent closed his eyes for a moment to compose himself. "Our competitors have already introduced newer versions of their software. We're at least six months behind."

He turned to Venkat Iyengar, the VP of engineering, and said, "Our product cycle is getting longer. I've been asking for a few features in the interim that will help us close some of the deals in our pipeline. Why are we dragging our feet?"

"We're working hard to accommodate the sales team's requests," replied Venkat. "But every feature we work on, delays the next full version. Many of these interim features violate the user interface design." He paused for a second, rubbing his forehead with slender fingers. "I have tried my best to understand why these features are so important."

Barry began to say something when Trent turned to him and said, "All I'm saying is you hired me two years ago, and I'm the reason why Hintec started growing again. The sales team delivered last year, but it's been back breaking to compensate for our poor customer retention."

Trent looked around the table at his colleagues. "It's January and I can already tell, this year I'll need serious help from all of you, from marketing and engineering to customer service, to produce new sales growth again."

Barry sighed. "Let's make sure your desire for growth doesn't put Hintec in jeopardy by overextending ourselves.

We want growth, but not at the cost of profitability. As Hector said, we can enhance customer service, but it will cost us far more. We can speed up product development, but again, it will affect the bottom line. Your team needs to sell the product we have now, and set the right expectations with customers."

Trent glanced towards the VP of HR and the CFO seated on the other end of the table. Neither responded, and Barry moved on to the next agenda item.

That night after dinner, Trent and his wife Lori retired to their large master bedroom. She leaned back against the pillows on their king-sized bed and opened the stocks investment book she had been reading. Trent lay on his back beside her, tracing the line of white crown molding that surrounded the vaulted ceiling. He shifted his gaze toward Lori. He could see her face partially hidden by the book. Long lashes surrounded her big eyes, and brunette hair cascaded down her shoulders. He smiled.

Just then, his Blackberry vibrated. He picked it up from the nightstand, checked the new e-mail, and put it down. "That was Barry," he said turning to Lori, "it's time for him to step down. I think the board members are getting restless."

Lori lay her book aside and looked at him.

"Are they ready to make a change?" she enquired.

"At least three board members have had lunch with me. None of them said it was an interview, but I figure they're meeting with the management team members to determine who'd be the best to lead Hintec."

"Will they hire someone as young as you to be CEO?"

"Sure, why not? Wasn't Bob, the president at the bank you worked for in San Jose, quite young?"

Lori worked as a HR director before their son was born. She was now a homemaker and spent her time taking care of their investments.

She shrugged, "Bob was in his late-forties and had been with the bank for twenty years. You're 39 and look even younger." She smiled as she looked into his shapely, greenish grey eyes.

Trent didn't smile back. Running his hand through his dark brown hair, he said, "Age won't be an issue. They recognize I'm brilliant and not just a pretty face. Hintec needs new energy at the top. Barry's become lazy. He should retire and go enjoy the ton of money he's made."

Trent spent the week working on sales activities. On Friday morning, he was in his office working on a proposal when his telephone rang. He answered the phone.

"Trent, this is Cedric. Would you please come to the boardroom?"

Cedric Haker was the chairman and founder of Hintec.

"I'll be right there," Trent responded.

At the boardroom, he pushed the door gently and entered. All the nine board members, including CEO Barry Elrod were in the room. Trent nodded in greeting and took a seat.

Seated at the far end of the table, Cedric welcomed him and smiled. "Trent, we met this morning to discuss the appointment of a new CEO."

Trent's heart skipped a beat.

"The board has elected to appoint you. Congratulations!"

Trent's eyes twinkled and his heart beat faster.

Cedric continued, "Barry will stay on the board and has agreed to be available as an advisor to you and the team."

Trent nodded. After Cedric adjourned the meeting, the board members including Barry walked over to shake Trent's hand and congratulate him. Trent smiled broadly.

As everyone began to leave, Barry turned to Trent and in a rejected tone offered, "I'll move my things out today, so if you like, you can move into my office over the weekend."

"Thanks, Barry," said Trent with half-a-smile.

After the others left, Cedric sat down at the head of the table and asked Trent to join him. Cedric, 66 years old, started Hintec when he was 55. He was the CFO at a company before he had the idea to form Hintec. The name Hintec was a short form of Houston business-intelligence technologies.

Cedric had hired Barry as his VP of engineering to build the software. When Cedric retired, he picked Barry to replace him as CEO. That was five years ago.

"Cedric, I really appreciate this," said Trent, sitting down.

Cedric patted Trent's shoulder. "You're the right person for the job. I'll ask Maxell to send out a press release by noon today. But first, you and I need to agree on your compensation."

After they discussed the package, Cedric asked, "Does that sound good?"

"Yes, indeed. Thank you very much," said Trent.

Cedric had a flight to catch. They shook hands and walked out of the boardroom.

As soon as Cedric turned the corner, Trent gave a victory punch in the air and raced back to his office. He stopped by his assistant, Amy Reiter, whose cubicle was outside his office. Assuming a serious expression, he said, "I'm afraid you have a new role. You'll be working for the CEO from now on."

Amy, in her late twenties, looked puzzled and frowned. "Why…," she began and then looked at Trent's beaming face. "Is that right? Wow!"

"Yes, I'm now the CEO!" He threw his fists up in the air.

"Congratulations!"

"Thanks."

She got up and gave him a quick hug.

"Boy, will Lori be excited," he said grinning.

"Are you going to call her?"

"No, I'm going to wait till I get home. I want to see the look on her face."

Amy smiled. She had been his assistant since he had joined Hintec. She liked working for him and was loyal to him.

Several management team members came to congratulate Trent after the announcement went out. Hector, the COO, and Maxell, the VP of marketing, were not among them.

After lunch, Simon Woods, the director of sales, knocked. Trent had hired Simon ten months ago. Simon was the same age as Trent but had spent fewer years in sales than Trent had.

"Come in," said Trent.

Simon entered and closed the door behind him. As he sat down, he said, "I just got back from my lunch appointment. Congratulations! This is great news. Finally, Barry's out of the way! Now we can make the changes we want."

"I'm not sure how involved Barry will be," Trent responded. "He's still a board member."

"How did you beat Hector? Wasn't he the CEO-in-waiting?"

"I can't imagine them considering him. Customer service has so many issues. I wonder what Cedric has in mind for Hector."

"You're the CEO. Shouldn't it be your decision?"

"I wish it were that simple," Trent shrugged.

"So, do I become the new VP of sales?"

Trent burst out laughing. "You are subtle, aren't you? Don't worry, Simon, I'll take care of you."

Looking at his watch, Trent said, "I better get back to work. I have a lot on my plate to finish this afternoon."

In the evening, Trent pulled beneath his home's two-story porte cochere, sprang out of his car, and rang the doorbell in rapid succession. He peaked in through the twelve-foot, crystal glass, double doors. They lived in a suburb of Houston, Texas, and their home backed up to a seventy-acre, man-made lake.

"Mommy, its Daddy," yelled Ethan, their three-year old son as he ran up to the door. Lori followed him and opened the door. "Why didn't you come in through the garage as you always do? What's this in your hand?"

Trent placed the box he was holding on the side table. He grabbed Lori and gave her a passionate kiss. After they finished kissing, she pulled back. "What's going on?"

"I have great news!! I'm now the CEO!"

"Oh, my God!" she said and hugged him.

Ethan watched all of this a little dumbstruck.

"Daddy's now the big dog!" said Trent, turning to Ethan.

Ethan looked puzzled. "Daddy's a dog?"

Lori and Trent laughed.

"Oh, oh... oh, my," said Lori. "I felt a little butterfly in my stomach. The baby's moving!"

Trent smiled. They walked into the family room and Lori sat down on the couch. She took Ethan's hand and pressed it against her stomach. He giggled. "When can I see the baby?"

"In five months," said Lori.

Trent fetched the box he had brought. Giving it to Lori, he said, "It's the fine chocolate you like."

"Is it candy? Open it. Open it," insisted Ethan as he hopped in excitement. Trent picked up Ethan and swung him around. It was a perfect moment of happiness.

That night as Trent lay on the bed looking at the ceiling Lori snuggled next to him and put her arm around him.

"Are we purchasing a minivan this weekend?" she asked.

"Yes," he replied. "I'll go by the office early in the morning so I can move some of my important stuff into my new office, and there's some work I need to finish."

"Okay," she said, "Ethan and I can meet you when you're done, and we can go from there."

He nodded and said, "I'm excited. I feel I can make anything happen. I want to take Hintec to new heights."

She smiled and hugged him tightly.

"I have a lot to think about. How should I take Hintec in a new direction? What should I fix? And, I have a lot of sales pressure this quarter."

Early Saturday morning, Trent raced his silver BMW from his home toward uptown Houston, his mind full of thoughts. He walked into Hintec's offices on the 20th floor of the green glass high-rise, and headed straight for his new office.

He entered a room, twice the size of his old office. It surrounded him with a panoramic view of the city. As he walked toward the window, he could see the sunrise behind the cluster of downtown buildings, five miles east. South of downtown, he could see the football stadium against the horizon and below him, the cars on the crisscrossing network of freeways. It was as if Houston was coming alive for him before his eyes. He felt on top of the world.

On Sunday night, he walked into his closet to lay out clothes for his first day as CEO. He picked out a white shirt, black suit and a bright, colorful tie that was his hallmark. When he came out of the closet, he said to Lori who was sitting on the bed, "If I do even half the job Barry was doing, Hintec will go places."

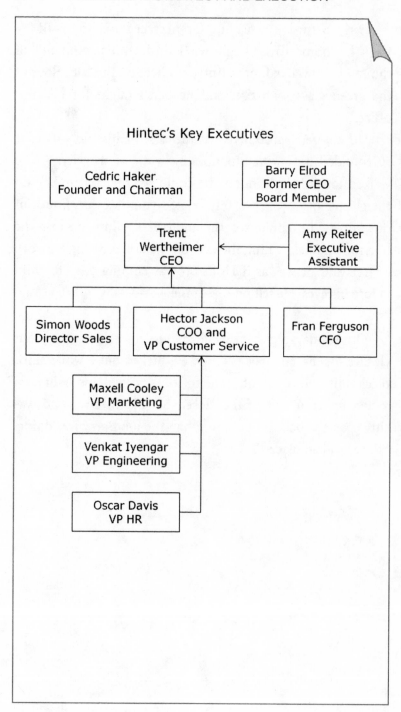

Hintec's Key Executives

Chapter 2: Tribulations

On Monday morning, Trent arrived for the management meeting a few minutes before the scheduled time and sat at the head of the table.

Maxell, the VP of marketing, arrived second. He sat down three chairs away from Trent and offered half-hearted congratulations. Trent gave him a perfunctory thank you.

Fran, the CFO, Venkat, the VP of engineering, and Oscar, the VP of HR, walked in soon after.

"It's five past 9:00 AM, let's get started," said Trent.

Hector, the COO, walked in.

Trent acknowledged him with a nod. "As your new CEO, I look forward to working with you to take Hintec to the next level. Instead of a long agenda, I wanted a quick meeting to thank you for your congratulations and early offers of support."

"What were the criteria?" interjected Hector.

"Criteria for what?" asked Trent, unsure about the question.

"Criteria for selecting the CEO," replied Hector firmly.

Trent bristled. "Why don't you ask the board?"

Oscar, fulfilling his role as VP of HR, jumped in. "The board made its decision. Let's respect it and work as a team."

"I second that," said Fran.

Maxell and Venkat didn't comment. Oscar looked at Hector. Finally, Hector said, "Okay, let's get on with the meeting."

"What is Barry's role going to be?" asked Maxell.

"He will continue as an advisor," Trent said.

"What does that mean?" needled Maxell.

"What it usually means," replied Trent, annoyed.

Undeterred, Maxell probed, "What changes are you planning?"

"I will share them in the next meeting." Turning to the others, Trent asked, "Other questions?" He waited a few moments for a response, and then said, "We all have a lot to get done; so let's go make it happen."

He watched as Hector and Maxell walked out of the room, talking to each other. He sighed.

The Chairman was back from his trip on Wednesday. Trent caught him in the hallway. "Do you have time to visit?" asked Trent.

"Sure," said Cedric.

They went to Trent's office, closed the door, and sat down.

"I have several questions."

"Sure," said Cedric, "things happened so quickly I didn't even talk to you before I announced you as the new CEO."

"I was wondering about that."

"My challenge was Barry," said Cedric shaking his head slightly. "It was time for him to step down, but he was vacillating. That morning, as soon as he became agreeable, I called you in because I didn't want him to change his mind."

Trent nodded, beginning to understand what had transpired.

"As you know, last year, I reduced my ownership to 43%. The two private equity firms now own slightly over 20% each. They wanted a change."

I can see why, thought Trent, but he didn't say anything.

Cedric continued, "I agreed because economic conditions are now right for pursuing growth. Barry produced no growth in his first year, and revenues declined the following two years."

Trent was familiar with the history, but he let Cedric recount it.

Cedric looked afar. "Economic conditions weren't good." He returned his gaze to Trent, and came a little closer. "But I feel Barry wasn't interested. Hintec was profitable, and Barry was making good money because we had designed his compensation to reward profitability. He focused only on costs and took his eyes off the other areas. The product cycles have become longer, and customer retention has been declining steadily. That's part of the reason we decided not to appoint Hector as CEO."

Trent was happy to get the scoop. He listened intently.

"Hiring you changed things, at least in the area of sales. And, the last two years, we saw a healthy growth in new sales."

Trent smiled lifting his head in pride.

"I'm a firm believer in promoting from within. Among the management team, the board sees you as the dynamic leader who can lead the company on a growth path for the next decade."

"I'm grateful for their vote of confidence."

Cedric pursed his lips. "There was push back that you are not ready, and your relationships with the other management members are a bit strained. But all the members like your energy and passion. You have a sharp mind and they expect you to grow in the role. Produce results and our faith will be vindicated."

"I will," said Trent with a resolute expression on his face. "Do I have the authority to make changes without oversight from Barry?"

"Sure, but use him as an advisor. I've asked him to visit with you to help with the transition."

Trent showed no reaction even though he didn't like the idea of taking advice from Barry. He went on to his next question, "Should we promote Simon to VP sales?"

"That's your decision."

Trent was happy to hear that and it gave him the encouragement to ask, "What about Hector?" He carefully watched Cedric's reaction.

Cedric turned sober. "It's important to understand the organization before making big changes. Give Hector the time to recognize you are the right leader for Hintec. Use your influence, not your authority to bring him in the fold."

The next morning, Trent's assistant, Amy, walked into his office. "Barry is available tomorrow to visit with you," she said.

"Put him off till next week," he said as he waved his hand. "I need to work on my presentation for the management meeting."

"Also," said Amy, "you have a meeting this afternoon with the prospect you met last week, and the big proposal meeting tomorrow afternoon."

"Yes, I'm preparing for it," acknowledged Trent.

On Monday morning, Trent arrived in the conference room for the management meeting. Once everyone sat down, he began, "Today's agenda is to go over the changes we need to make."

Hector, the COO, asked, "What's your philosophy behind the changes?"

"Driving growth. That's what the board wants." He turned to Maxell, "And to answer Maxell's question from last week, Barry will serve in an advisory role only. I have complete authority."

Trent turned to the others, and continued, "Our foremost issue is our clients aren't receiving the service they deserve or expect. It's the reason our customer retention rate is suffering."

Hector winced. In addition to his duties as COO, customer service was his directly responsibility. It was near and dear to him.

Trent noticed the frown on Hector's puckered face. "Let me go through the entire presentation," he said. "Then we can hear any counter-points. We haven't trained our customer service reps well. Once we train them better, they'll respond faster, and provide the necessary level of support. Second, our software lacks the features to wow prospects."

Trent looked at the VP of engineering. "Simon will give you an updated list of features. Implementing the features in the list is a much higher priority than working on the next version of the software."

Venkat dropped his shoulders.

Turning to the CFO, he said, "We need to produce aggressive growth. We grew last year by 10%, and this year, I'd like to target 20% growth. That means we must end the year with revenues of $240 million."

Fran digested what he had said, and asked, "Is that realistic?"

"It's a big challenge but achievable. When I started, Hintec had shrunk for two years. 10% annual growth seemed liked a huge jump, but I made it happen last year," he said, lifting his head and broadening his shoulders. "To produce growth, we will need more salespeople. In order to maintain the overall expenses, we'll reduce costs in other areas. See where we can trim the workforce and cut other costs."

Turning back toward Maxell, he said, "I'm putting an immediate freeze on consultants. You've engaged several in marketing, and, Fran, you've been using external accounting help as well. Let's bring the cost run-rate under control."

"I can't just fire them overnight," protested Maxell.

"Why not?" pushed Trent.

Maxell chose not to engage. Trent continued, "Our vision should be a lean machine, creating maximum value for our clients so we can produce the growth the board expects." Waving his index finger, he added, "It's about execution. Let's act as a team and make it happen."

Turning to Oscar, the VP of HR, Trent said, "Last but not least, communication is the best way to increase collaboration. I'll start sending a business-update email to all employees every Friday. I'll also hold monthly town hall meetings called, I'll-bring-sandwiches-you-bring-your-questions."

He looked around the table, "Any questions?"

Only Oscar spoke. Running his hand over his bald head, he said, "That's a lot."

"No, kidding," said Trent, and adjourned the meeting.

He stopped by Amy's cubicle on his way back to his office. "Can you set up meetings with Oscar and Fran?"

"Sure. Also, I've set up Barry's meeting for tomorrow."

"Okay," he said and walked into his office.

"How're things going?" asked Barry, the former CEO, when he came for the meeting.

"Quite well," said Trent, and invited Barry to sit down. "What have you heard?"

"Oh, nothing much," said Barry. "What's on our agenda?"

Trent narrowed his eyebrows. "You tell me. Sounds like Cedric and you talked about this meeting."

"Cedric asked me to be available to you in case you have questions or need my help," said Barry.

"Things are fine. Everyone is plugging along."

"Sounds like I'm of no help to you," joked Barry, but got no response from Trent. "What about Hector and Maxell?"

Trent fidgeted. "You tell me."

"They're unsure about the approach."

Trent turned stern.

"You must find a way to include them," advised Barry. "They're now part of your team."

"I will, but they've to get on the bandwagon. I must figure out how to make that happen," said Trent, searching his mind for a solution.

"If you need me to talk to them, I'll be more than happy to."

"I appreciate your offer. I'll let you know," said Trent, unsure if he wanted Barry's help.

"I'm also stepping down from the board," said Barry. "It's important for you to have all the room you need to run Hintec in the way you want."

"Thank you, Barry," said Trent, with a broad smile, surprised and pleased.

Trent met with the VP of HR later that afternoon. Oscar Davis had been with Hintec since inception and had the respect of the employees and the management team. Cedric and Oscar had worked together before Cedric founded Hintec. Oscar was in his late fifties.

"I'd like to promote Simon to VP of sales," Trent began as soon as Oscar sat down.

"Is he the best candidate?"

"He's all we have. He's been here over a year, and it's worked out well," justified Trent.

"Should we consider external candidates?"

Trent shook his head. "I don't want to go through a lengthy process."

"Okay," said Oscar, dissatisfied, but accepting Trent's decision to move quickly.

"Changing subjects, what's our current headcount?"

"Just over eleven hundred," replied Oscar.

"We should look at reducing that by 8 to 10%."

Oscar's brow furrowed. "Why do we need to cut back?"

"To meet our growth goal, we need to double our sales force," Trent said, pursuing the line of reasoning he had formulated earlier. "Good salespeople are expensive; to maintain expenses, we must cut jobs from the other areas."

Oscar ran his hand over his bald head a couple of times and then said, "Cutting jobs should be carried out after careful consideration." He looked at Trent with a concerned expression. "I am not against it, but, if the cuts aren't presented right, they won't help the company."

Trent nodded accepting his point. "If you present the message and deliver the news, it will be well received."

When Oscar hesitated, Trent added, "If you're uncomfortable, I'll deliver the news. Of course, we aren't going to do anything immediately." He paused. "But, hiring additional salespeople is a high priority. Let's start by promoting Simon. Please put together a package similar to the one I negotiated. I want to take care of Simon, but create a package that rewards him only if he generates aggressive sales growth. Fran can help you with some of the performance metrics."

Oscar nodded, still thoughtful.

"Okay," Trent said, "What else is happening in the company? What are people saying to you about my promotion?"

"The employees are okay; they aren't affected. Hector and Maxell are concerned about the changes."

Trent drew a deep breath. "Hector will resist change no matter what. He's unwilling to admit we have so many issues. And, he hasn't pushed Venkat." He shook his head. "Maxell on the other hand isn't adding value."

Trent looked away to think for a moment, and then surmised, "Venkat and Maxell report to Hector. That's why we have all these problems. I'll reorganize our team. It will increase accountability and light a fire under everyone's feet."

"What're you planning?" asked Oscar a little alarmed.

"I'll let you know the details soon," said Trent, not wanting to reveal his plans.

Oscar decided against pushing any further.

The following Monday, Oscar dropped off Simon's offer letter. After reviewing it, Trent called the director of sales, and asked him to come see him.

"Good morning," said Simon as he walked in.

"Would you please get the door?"

"Sure," said Simon. He closed the door and took a seat.

"Congratulations, you're the new VP of sales!"

"Wow! You're a man of action!"

"You deserve it," said Trent. "Here's your offer letter and compensation package. Oscar put it together, so, if you like it, the credit goes to him. I'm sure you will. It's a great package."

"I love working for you, you can make people feel special."

"Quit sucking up. You already have the promotion."

"No, I mean it," said Simon emphatically.

"Well, I wouldn't rejoice just yet. The package is great, but you get the big bucks only if you deliver growth. Now, you have to make it happen, and I'm sure you will do a fantastic job."

The phone rang. Trent answered. "It's time for the management meeting," said Amy.

He turned around to look at the time on the computer. "Oh, thank you," he said. "Simon and I'll leave right away."

They both walked out of the office, Simon with a big grin.

When Trent and Simon walked into the conference room, everyone else was already present. Trent sat down and started, "We must focus like a laser and move at breakneck speed." With an air of confidence, he said, "Because of all that we need to do, I've decided to reorganize." He looked around at the expectant faces. "I've promoted Simon to VP sales, and I invited him to join our management meeting."

Everyone applauded and congratulated Simon.

After the applause subsided, Trent turned toward Hector and said, "Since we have so many customer service issues, I ask you to concentrate only on that area. Maxell, Oscar and Venkat, will report to me directly."

Hector stared icily at Trent.

"None of this was discussed with me," said Maxell forcefully as he looked at Oscar. "Obviously, Hector didn't know either." He looked at Fran and Venkat. "Did you know about these changes?"

"Maxell," Trent said firmly, "the old structure is inefficient."

Shaking his head, Maxell said, "We can't roll-out new roles and responsibilities without first discussing it and evaluating its impact."

Trent raised his palm to counter him. "I won't have an organization that spends all its time in discussion. These changes are here to stay, period."

"What do you expect of us?" asked Venkat in a low tone.

"I'll visit with each of you to discuss the details," said Trent, not wanting to get into an extended discussion.

Wanting to figure out a way to work with the VP of Marketing, Trent scheduled a meeting with Maxell. When Maxell walked in, Trent greeted him. "Good morning, Maxell."

"Morning," replied Maxell curtly as he sat down.

"It's clear to me you're not a big fan of me or my changes… especially the part about reporting to me directly," said Trent addressing the issue head-on.

"I like reporting to Hector, we have a great relationship. He recognizes I'm the marketing guru and lets me do my thing. He appreciates the value the marketing team creates," asserted Maxell.

"Are you truly creating value? Are you, really?" said Trent, bearing down on Maxell.

"What do you mean?" pushed back Maxell in an angry voice. "I realize the sales team thinks we're overhead and only they create value," he said throwing his hands up in the air.

The 33 years old, lanky, VP of marketing was a firm believer in the creative side of marketing. He loved to dabble with things on the leading edge of marketing. Social media was his latest focus.

Unfazed by Maxell's anger, Trent said, "Please don't tell me re-doing the website created value, and I hope you realize re-coloring brochures doesn't increase sales."

Maxell shifted uncomfortably. "Trent, the concepts and techniques of marketing are changing rapidly. Unless, we keep up, we'll become dinosaurs. We have differences because you belong to a different era and don't trust my judgment."

"I'm not a dinosaur and neither is Hintec," said Trent, taking offence. "The most important thing is marketing ROI. I can't tell the ROI on the ads you run. Our prospects don't remember seeing our ads. Do we have the right message? Are you sure we're targeting the right media?" rattled off Trent, challenging Maxell's assertions.

The dimpled chin Maxell looked completely stunned. His furtive eyes looked away from Trent.

Trent got up from his seat and walked over to the window while Maxell continued to sit in his chair. After a few minutes, Trent walked back and sat down, hands flat on the desk. "Maxell, the marketing and sales teams need to work hand-in-hand. Can we do that?"

"Yes," said Maxell without making eye contact.

Leaning forward, Trent said, "Your team can help us do the marketing research and help us position the product for the future. You can help the sales team with initial research on prospects, put together sales presentations and other marketing collaterals, and help develop proposals. Can you transition from creative to practical marketing?"

Maxell didn't say anything.

"Please work with Simon. Can you work with him?"

"Yes," said Maxell, this time looking at Trent.

"Thank you, Maxell. I appreciate it."

After Maxell left, Trent leaned back in his chair, wondering if he could count on Maxell to deliver what he needed to drive sales.

Trent met with the CFO to get an update on the financials. After Fran finished, Trent said, "You're doing an excellent job. I like your organized approach. Hintec is lucky to have you."

In her early forties, Fran Ferguson had joined Hintec a year ago, after a fast career track with another hi-tech company. She was an expert in the area of finance and accounting, measured and professional in her demeanor.

"Thank you," said Fran, enjoying the compliment, as she pushed her black, shoulder-length hair, behind her ear.

"I wish new sales were doing as well," lamented Trent. "My becoming CEO isn't helping the sales pipeline. I hope promoting Simon to VP sales will get sales back on track."

"That's a good move," endorsed Fran.

"I've asked him to aggressively hire salespeople."

"That will impact payroll costs," cautioned Fran.

"I realize that. That's why I need your help in identifying the areas in which we can cut fat."

"The functional heads have a better sense of that."

"But they won't volunteer. You, Oscar, and I have to devise the game plan. Hector, Maxell and Venkat will resist."

"I would involve them early so you can get their buy-in," she advised, adjusting her rimless glasses.

"Their buy-in will be a huge challenge," he said discounting her advice. Looking squarely at her, he said, "I'd be remiss if I didn't ask you to reduce headcount in your area."

"I'll look into it," she promised.

Continuing his series of meetings with the team members, Trent met with the VP of engineering the next day. He started, "Venkat, I realize you had a close relationship with Barry."

"Yes," said the 36 year old. "Barry and I did the programming for the earlier versions of our software, basically, laying its foundation. I've a lot of respect for him. I worked for him for nine years."

Barry had hired Venkat soon after Venkat graduated with his masters. Venkat had emigrated from India for higher studies. Barry liked Venkat's intelligence, sincerity, and work ethic. When Barry became CEO, he appointed Venkat as the VP of engineering.

"Now, it's you and me," said Trent, looking to build a relationship.

"I'll do everything I can to make you happy," said Venkat, ever looking to please.

"That's what I was looking for," said Trent smiling. Returning to his agenda, he said, "You realize we need several features implemented quickly."

Venkat's discomfort showed clearly on his slender face. "I... I felt, and Barry felt the same way... that in a way...."

"You don't have to hesitate," said Trent to reassure him.

The medium built Venkat mustered enough courage to say, "In the engineering team we feel we're the punching bag. If the sales team doesn't close the deals, we're blamed."

Trent didn't take it well. He winced.

"I didn't mean to offend you," said Venkat seeing Trent's reaction.

"I realize there are two ways to look at the same issue," said Trent, searching for common ground. "We... I say we, I mean the sales team must communicate better. Their requests shouldn't be seen as an excuse for non-performance."

"I didn't mean it that way," said Venkat defensively.

Trent waved his hand, "Don't worry about it." The six feet CEO got up, came around the desk, and put his hand on Venkat's shoulder. "You and your team are the heart of Hintec. Without you, we have nothing."

Venkat nodded, appreciating the reassurance. Trent walked back to his seat and sat down. He leaned forward, and said, "The two of us need to be on the same team."

"I'm with you," reiterated Venkat.

"Good," said Trent. "Now, may we talk about the features?"

They discussed further and then concluded the meeting.

Meeting with the VP of customer service was next on the list. Trent wasn't looking forward to the meeting.

"Good morning," said Hector as he came in at the scheduled time.

"Good morning. Thanks for coming," responded Trent.

"Sure thing," said Hector as he sat down.

Trent figured he'd address the elephant in the room, and in a measured manner said, "I can appreciate you being upset about not being appointed CEO."

"Wait a minute," said a startled Hector. "Who told you I was upset about not becoming CEO?"

"You're not?" asked a bewildered Trent.

"No. I questioned the process because the board should've done a better job of communicating the process. It was secretive, as if they were afraid of something. That was a wrong message to send to top executives," said the 55 year old Hector.

"I can see that," said Trent agreeing with Hector.

In his career of 35 years, Hector had primarily worked in roles with a heavy operational focus. He had worked hard to become COO, and had not forgiven Trent for demoting him from COO to VP of customer service.

"In any case, that's water under the bridge," said Hector. "You know, I'm always forthright. Your management style upsets me. You behave like a know-it-all. The rest of us have a lot of experience. You forget we brought Hintec to this level."

Even though he was used to Hector's brusque mannerisms, Trent didn't appreciate Hector's tone. He pushed his chair back and raised his eyebrows, wondering how to respond.

Hector was just getting started. "I'm tired of your complaints. Under the circumstances, we've done a great job. Our product is complex and understandably our customers have a difficult time utilizing it."

Trent tried to interject but Hector didn't let him. He pointed his finger at Trent. "You don't understand our customers. What they go through and how they use our product. Because you've closed a few deals, you believe you understand everything. I...."

"That's enough," forcefully interrupted Trent holding his palm up. "I know what our customers want. You may not respect me and you may not respect selling, but the fact is you can never sell if you don't understand the customer."

Pointing his finger back at Hector, Trent said, "The real issue is you have no appreciation for customer service, and Barry didn't hold you accountable. I won't operate the way he did. I strongly recommend you get your act together, and fast."

"Don't worry about me. Now, I only have to take care of customer service. It will be the best performing area."

Trent took several deep breaths after Hector left, his head spinning.

That evening, Lori and Trent sat on their back porch. He lit the fire pit, and they warmed their hands over it. Ethan watched TV inside.

"How're things at work?" asked Lori.

"It's difficult to get the organization to go through changes. I wish I had a magic wand I could wave."

"Me too. I wish I had a magic wand so I wouldn't have to go through the nine months of pregnancy."

"Okay, I won't whine. I don't know what else to do but to push the management team even more to make things happen."

When he arrived the next morning, his assistant was already at her desk. After greeting her, he said, "Please schedule town-hall lunch meetings where we can invite large groups of employees."

"The lunch room seats fifty," said Amy.

"That will work."

"When?"

"Starting in a couple of weeks." He looked at the calendar on her computer, and said, "Book the second and fourth Fridays of February and March."

On Monday, Trent received Simon's e-mail with the sales report for January. He picked up the phone and called the VP of sales. "I want to attend your sales meeting."

"Is everything okay?" asked Simon a little nervous.

"The pipeline isn't looking good," said a concerned Trent. "We're in the sixth week of the quarter. We have to hustle to make these deals happen."

Simon hesitated. "But we have $46 million in this quarter's pipeline. If we assume an 80% success rate, like we always do, we will comfortably be at our goal of $35 million."

"No. No. The pipeline is misleading," stressed Trent. "It's loaded with large deals. Be careful, these aren't easy deals. If they don't close, we could miss the quarter by a wide margin. Stay focused and push really hard," said Trent emphatically.

"I will," assured Simon.

The following week Oscar came to see Trent. After the VP of HR sat down, he handed Trent a sheet of paper.

"Here's the latest version of the staff reduction plan. The total in this version is 50 employees, or 4.5% of the workforce. As you requested, most of the reductions came from customer service and engineering. Marketing will reduce by nine employees, which is 30% of that department. That makes marketing's reduction the biggest in percentage. Finance has agreed to reduce by two and so will HR."

Trent read the document. "Put it in motion. I need the reduction done by the end of February, so I can share the payroll savings for March with the board in the April meeting. They'll be pleased."

"Are you really sure about the reductions?" quizzed Oscar, as he ran his hand over his bald head. "You realize you're forcing your wishes on your team. This won't help your relationships," he warned.

"I realize that, Oscar," said Trent thoughtfully. "But it's the right thing to do for Hintec. I also recognize it is people's lives, but unfortunately, it's necessary."

Three weeks passed. The downsizing was carried out and fifty employees were let go.

In the second week of March, Trent was working in his office when Amy called. "Simon is here. He wants to see you."

"Send him in. Why's he asking? He can just knock."

"I have bad news," said the VP of sales as he entered.

"Are you quitting?" said Trent sitting up.

"No. I might be fired, though," said Simon as he stood looking at Trent.

"What're you talking about?" said Trent irritated.

"Wesley Chemicals terminated our relationship."

Trent stood up and gave a hard push to his chair. "That's our biggest client. What did you do? I gave you that account so you could grow it, not lose it," he said, banging his hand on the wall cabinet. "I've had that relationship for two years with no problems."

"I know," said Simon sheepishly, standing across the desk from Trent. "I told the CIO how much we value them. George said things were out of his control. He couldn't convince his management they needed to continue to spend on our software, given their recent focus on cost control."

"Don't they see the value of using the software?"

"He said their management thinks software such as ours really doesn't create value."

"What a load of crap! I'll give him a call. They invested $21 million in the original deal. How can they just walk away?"

"George said their CFO balked at spending $5 million for new licenses in addition to the $3 million they spend on annual maintenance. George said he doesn't want us to bother him. He has nothing further to discuss."

"Simon, you're killing me. I don't believe this. How can this relationship change so drastically? Schedule an emergency sales meeting for after-hours tonight."

Simon assembled the salespeople who were in town in the conference room. The others joined by phone. Trent opened, "Simon gave me the wonderful news about Wesley

Chemicals. Let's go through the pipeline and see where we stand. If I get any sandbagging, I will shoot you."

After the review, Trent was fuming. "Simon assured me things are under control. Our goal this quarter was $35 million. According to all of you, we'll barely reach $23 million. This is just perfect. What fantastic news to share at the board meeting."

After the sales team left, Trent pulled Simon aside. "I should fire you. You told me we would make the $35 million goal."

"We would, if the $5 million from Wesley and a couple of other deals had come in. I didn't learn those wouldn't close until this meeting," mumbled Simon looking down at his feet.

On the second Friday in April, Cedric began the board meeting, "We have several items on the agenda. To start, Trent will give us an update on the first quarter."

Seated across from Cedric, Trent said, "The last quarter was my first quarter as CEO. We implemented many changes. First, we brought costs under control by reducing staff."

Several board members nodded approval. He continued, "We are aggressively pursuing growth and have spent considerable time searching for top-notch sales talent. We intend to double the sales team."

"How are renewals and sales?" asked Cedric.

"It was a challenging quarter. One of our big clients, Wesley Chemicals, chose not to renew. We were looking to up-sell additional licenses to them. As a result of that and other challenges, our numbers are not what I would have liked."

Looking at the board members, he said, "We expect to be within 5% of our renewal targets at the end of the year. New sales for this quarter were $23 million."

"What was our goal for the quarter," asked John Summers, a board member representing RiverRock Funds, one of the private equity groups.

"$35 million."

"What did we do last year in the same quarter?" asked John.

"$22 million."

"Because our renewal rate is only 81%, don't new sales have to compensate for the lost 20%, and produce new growth?" pushed John.

"That's right," said Trent demurely.

"And we lost one of our biggest clients," said John unrelenting.

Trent tried to put up a defense, "We have implemented a lot of changes, and we need to make a lot of improvements. Changes are going to cause bumps in the road."

"Is losing the biggest client just a bump?" asked John in a challenging tone. "What is the reason?"

"Poor customer service," replied Trent.

John probed further, "What changes in customer service have you implemented?"

"The most important change was reorganizing the management team. Hector, who had multiple responsibilities as COO, is now solely responsible for customer service. He is dedicating himself completely to improving that area."

"But you reduced staff from customer service?" pushed John.

"Yes, twenty positions."

John looked questioningly at Trent. "If customer service is your biggest challenge, why did you reduce their staff? Shouldn't you help that area before hiring more salespeople? Why hire more sales staff? Is your assumption that your salespeople are at maximum productivity? If you double the sales team, are you going to double the new sales goal?"

Trent didn't answer and looked at Cedric.

"John, it's early for us to be splitting hairs," said Cedric coming to Trent's rescue. "As a board, we don't want to second-guess our CEO. Let Trent work his changes, and then we can hold him accountable." Turning to Trent, Cedric said, "It is alarming to miss the quarterly goal and lose the biggest client. Let's make sure this one-time setback doesn't become a pattern."

"It won't," said Trent.

Cedric turned back to the rest of the board members and said with authority, "Trent helped acquire Wesley Chemicals in the first place. He turned around the sales team, and I'm sure he will successfully turn around all of Hintec." Looking at John, Cedric said, "Every CEO needs time to put his or her changes in place. We must give Trent the time, encouragement, and space to implement his changes."

Trent heaved a sigh of relief.

Trent spent the weekend regurgitating the board meeting in his mind. Seeing him in a pensive mood, Lori asked him, "Is something bothering you?"

"I've been thinking about what to do to turn things around," he confided. "My challenges are overwhelming. I figure, I have to work harder… at customer service, sales and engineering. Get beneath the surface, dig into the details, and find out what's really happening."

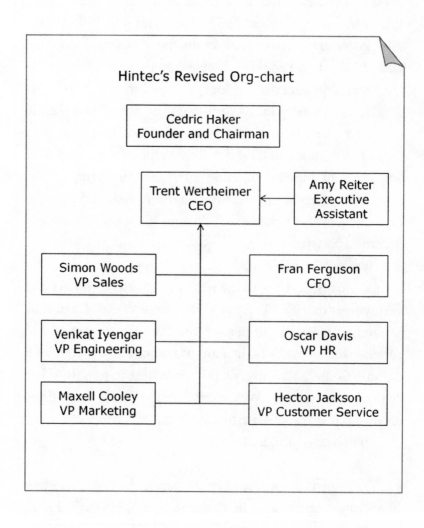

Chapter 3: Meltdown

In the management meeting on the following Monday, Trent began to explain his next steps, "I need better visibility. This morning, Fran and I developed a list of metrics we want to track. Sales pipeline metrics, marketing campaign effectiveness, customer service metrics, and, product cycle metrics: how fast we are developing features."

"How will you track marketing campaign effectiveness?" asked Maxell, wanting to find out how Trent was planning to measure marketing performance.

"I haven't thought that through. We'll figure it out," said Trent, not wanting to get in a detailed discussion at that point.

Venkat asked, "When you say how fast we're developing features, are you lumping all the features together regardless of complexity, and tracking the quantity of features developed."

"Guys," said Trent annoyed, "I'm sure we have to think more about this."

"This isn't a trivial task," said Maxell, not backing down. "Who's going to track these metrics and generate the reports?"

"Fran and her team are responsible for this project," replied Trent.

"I thought she was heavily staff-constrained," pushed Maxell. "Isn't that why more people weren't let go from the finance department?"

"We'll take care about resourcing the project," said Trent trying to cut off Maxell.

"Of course," retorted Maxell.

Trent moved on to the other agenda items.

After the meeting, the CFO stayed back to talk to Trent. "Resourcing is a challenge. My team is pushed to their limits."

"Let us hire a financial analyst," said Trent. "Drat, we let go two analysts from your area."

"We pushed through the staff reduction in haste," said Fran. "We should've considered it more carefully."

"I don't want to talk about what we could have or should have done. We should take the time to analyze this project, which will give us time between the reduction and the re-hiring."

Fran didn't look happy.

"Can we just leave it at that?" he asked.

"Sure, okay. I'm frustrated with our fickleness. Tracking metrics is a good idea, and we should implement it regardless of any political fallout. If we made a mistake in reducing staff in haste, that is all right," said Fran.

"We didn't make a mistake," said Trent, his face tightening. "We had fat in the system. There's a lot of complaining about the staff-reductions, but, if you notice, we're still able to get the same amount of work done."

Looking at his watch, he said, "We've gotten off topic. We need a better handle on what's happening. While we wait for the metrics project to come on-line, I'll get my hands dirty and jump into the customer service and engineering areas."

When Amy walked into her cubicle the next day, she found a big bouquet of flowers on her desk and a card from her boss, "Happy Birthday! Would you join me for lunch?"

She walked into Trent's office. "You're going through a lot right now. You shouldn't have worried about my birthday."

"I don't take the time to thank you. I'm sure you help me in ways I'll never know. I depend on you a lot."

Amy smiled and walked out. She was average looking, and didn't spend much time on dressing up. But it being a special day, she had worn a pretty dress.

They ate at an upscale restaurant close to the office. Trent ordered a blackened catfish and Amy ordered a chicken salad.

"You are looking good today," said Trent.

"Thank you," she said. "Thank you again for lunch."

"Oh, sure. So, what's the grapevine saying? What are people talking about?"

"Well initially, as I had shared with you before, there was uncertainty and fear about the staff reduction. Now, everyone knows we're done, and they aren't concerned."

After the management meeting the following Monday, Trent asked Simon to stay back. "I've been trying to figure out how to turnaround the ship. I researched the numbers. Our customer renewal rate has declined steadily for the last five years, from 93% down to 81%."

"I guess our customers stopped renewing because of poor service," deduced Simon.

"Let's keep a close eye on it. We need to turn it around."

The next day, the VP of sales walked into Trent's office. Trent looked up to see his pensive face.

"We lost another customer," said Simon anxiously.

"What! Which one?"

"Zucor Energy. They were acquired and didn't recommend us to the acquiring company."

"Why not?" asked Trent, gritting his teeth.

"They had trouble generating information. They asked for help, but in the end, felt like a football going between our different departments. They weren't able to get what they needed and it made them look bad to the acquiring company."

"I don't believe this. We need to get to the bottom of this," said Trent seething. "Call Hector. No, call Martha, the director who works for him. I think she handles the Tier 1 service calls."

When Martha walked in, Trent invited her to take a seat.

"What happened with Zucor Energy?" asked Trent hiding his ire. "They didn't recommend us to the company that acquired them."

"Is Hector joining us?" asked Martha looking around. "I didn't realize Zucor didn't recommend us. We did everything we could… we absolutely did."

"Martha, we just want to understand what happened," said Trent trying to calm her.

"It started with a Tier 1 call," explained Martha. "They complained a report wasn't working. We checked and found it was okay, but they still weren't happy and so after a few calls we escalated the issue to Tier 3 and turned it over to engineering."

"What happened then?" asked Trent.

"I don't know. Once it goes to engineering, they resolve the issue and close it out in the system."

"Don't you keep track to make sure the customer's needs have been met?" asked Simon.

Martha struggled. "We get a lot of calls, and we're maxed out, especially after the staff reduction. Once we turn it over to engineering, we don't have the time to go back and check. We know our engineers are the experts, and they'll solve the issue."

"Let's call Venkat," said Trent as he dialed the VP of engineering's extension. "Venkat, do you know about Zucor Energy's issue?"

After a pause, Venkat replied, "No, what's the issue?"

"That's what we're trying to find out. Can you come to my office and bring the director in-charge of the Tier 3 service calls?"

When Venkat walked in with Sam, Trent stood up from his desk and motioned everyone to sit at the round table closer to the window. Turning to Sam, Trent asked, "Do you know about Zucor Energy's service call?"

"Yes sir, I do," replied Sam.

"What do you know?"

"Their understanding of how our reports work was inaccurate."

"What do you mean?" asked Trent disturbed by the answer.

"Somehow they had the wrong notion. Our system's not designed to handle what they wanted."

"What could they have wanted that we can't handle?" asked Trent as he looked at Venkat.

Unperturbed, Sam replied, "I can explain, but it's technical."

"I can understand technical," snapped Trent.

Sam explained, "Cubes are data views, and you can't combine them across time in the way Zucor wanted. They must redesign their cubes, and collect data differently with a time dimension to it."

After thinking about it for a minute, Trent said, "Wait a minute, why did they think they could do it in the first place."

"I asked them that. They told me our sales staff told them we could do it."

"Who is the salesperson servicing Zucor?" asked Trent.

"It's Bob," replied the VP of sales.

Simon summoned Bob. All eyes were on him when he walked in. Trent motioned him to take a seat at the table.

"Bob, did you create an impression with Zucor Energy that we couldn't fulfill," asked Trent forcefully.

"No, not all," replied Bob. "They had asked me if they could get temporal information from our system. I told them, I'd have to check on it and get back to them. I called engineering and asked if we could. I was told, yes."

"Who did you talk to?" asked Trent.

"To one of the engineers who works for Sam."

Sam jumped in. "Sure, if you ask an engineer if we can retrieve temporal information, the answer is yes. But the client must collect it and configure it in the cubes. If they haven't done that, the reports can't magically produce that information."

Exasperated, Trent ran his hands through his hair. "I'm getting a headache," he said. "Why didn't you follow up to make sure the problem was resolved," he asked Bob. "Maybe if you had done so, we wouldn't have lost this client."

"I did follow up," protested Bob. "They had an issue with the report and were working with customer service. Finally, they told me they were unable to resolve the issue. I informed Simon that customer service had failed us once again."

Trent's expression changed as if he had seen a ghost. "Everyone except Simon, please leave," he said waving his hands.

Everyone got up and exited quickly.

Trent stood up and looked out the window. "We've been crying wolf, and it's come back to bite us." With a pained and angry look, he turned to Simon. "We didn't lose this customer because of our service department. We lost it because of Bob. He didn't stay on top of the issue. He was ready to place blame, happy to conclude it is a customer service problem."

Simon looked down at the table, afraid to say anything.

"I will kick myself, if I realize the service issues we've been complaining about have more to do with our sales team's lack of product knowledge. Make sure our salespeople understand what in the blazes they're selling and don't have this casual attitude toward customer needs."

That night Trent lay on the bed, staring at the ceiling.

"My perspective is changing," he shared.

"What do you mean?" asked Lori.

"When I was VP sales, I didn't care about the issues the other departments were facing. But today... I didn't think only about sales, I had the perspective of the entire company."

"Wouldn't every CEO do that?"

"Yes, I guess so. But it happened to me for the first time. I've begun to think like a CEO. As I look beneath the surface, I'm getting a better sense for the overall issues. I'll continue down this path. Meet with Hector and Venkat's teams to get a better feel."

Trent scheduled another meeting with Hector. When the VP of customer service walked in, Trent greeted him congenially and went right to the point, "I need greater visibility into the customer service area."

"Am I not allowing you to have that visibility?" asked Hector trying to better understand Trent's statement.

"I'm not complaining," clarified Trent. "All I want to know is how can I tell things are working well?"

"You ask me."

Trent cringed.

"That's right, you ask me and I'll tell you how it's going."

"So how are things going in your area?" asked Trent.

"You forced a staff-reduction, but people have stepped up. They're hardworking folks. I heard you've realized customer service isn't creating all the problems. Salespeople like Bob are helping screw up customer relationships."

Trent gave no reaction.

Hector softened his tone and said, "Listen, you and I want the same thing. We want the best customer service for our customers."

"You're right. We want the same thing," said Trent relaxing his face. "So how do we make it happen? I'd like to meet with your senior team so I can get a feel for their thinking."

"I can tell you their thinking, but I don't mind you meeting with them. I have nothing to hide."

"Thanks. Would you work with Amy to schedule it?"

"Sure. How soon would you like to have the meeting?"

"The sooner the better."

"Okay, I will set it up for after lunch today."

"That works for me," said Trent.

As they ate dinner that evening, Lori shared, "We have new neighbors, Martha and Watson Hughes. They are retirees and seem like nice people. You should stop by and say hello."

"I'm too busy right now. I met with Hector's team today, and I realized what I espouse as CEO and what happens on the ground are disconnected. I wish I could connect them. I keep thinking I'll be able to step in and fix things, but every issue I look at, only gets murkier. It's like a surgeon who cuts open the patient to find it's a real mess."

"Can we avoid the gory stuff? Remember, I'm pregnant. I don't want to hear about surgeries going wrong."

"I'm sorry."

"You need to communicate more. As they say, communicate, communicate, and communicate," Lori advised, striking her fork against her glass once for each repetition.

"I am communicating more, certainly with my direct reports. The challenge is reconciling competing priorities, clarifying the message and making sense of it all, so it fits together. I must figure out how to do that."

The next morning, Trent called Venkat. "We're scheduled to meet today. Invite your two directors as well."

"Is everything okay?"

"Yes. I figured it will give them a chance to visit with me."

"Okay. I wish we could include the directors who are in our Indian offices via a phone conference."

"We'll do a phone conference with them later."

An hour after Trent met with Venkat, Hector burst in. "I heard the engineering team had a meeting with you," he said.

Trent looked up at Hector. "Yes, they did."

"They're pretty stressed out," said Hector animatedly.

"Good, maybe it will produce some action."

"Trent, they want to implement the features, but some of the features seem ad-hoc. They can take long to implement, delay the next version, and not add value. In fact, they might compromise the design and complicate the user interface. All the engineers are asking for is an objective assessment," pleaded Hector.

"Is that a delaying tactic?" asked Trent sharply. "They should've asked Maxell for the market research four months ago when the sales team gave them the list. I won't allow us to become bureaucratic."

Hector glared at him.

His face turning red, Trent snarled, "Moreover, why are you involved? If they have an issue with me, they need to come to me directly. I don't want you acting as an intermediary."

Hector shook his head and left. Trent called the VP of engineering.

"Venkat, if you have an issue, talk to me. I don't want to find out from Hector what is going on in your head. Yes, I am being forceful, but I am sick of waiting for things."

"Trent, we need to think carefully before you force us to implement these features."

"Okay, I'll accept that. If the features compromise the system, or increase complexity, then you must proactively discuss it with the sales team. Avoiding the situation and hoping the requests will go away, isn't going to help either of us. If a feature doesn't make sense, I'll push back on the sales team."

Six weeks passed. Two days before the July board meeting, Trent was lying on the bed staring at the ceiling. Lori was lying down as well. "My relationships with Hector and Maxell continue to deteriorate. My challenges since I became CEO have been never-ending; I haven't made nearly the progress I had envisioned. It's driving me crazy. I'm really worried about the board meeting."

The phone rang. Lori picked it up. It was her mother, Debra.

"Hi Mom," said Lori. "Are you packed?"

"Yes," said Debra.

"Good. My friend Emily and I will meet you at the airport, tomorrow."

Trent gestured for the phone. Lori handed it to him.

"Hi Mom, this is Trent. How're you? How's California?"

"I'm fine, thanks," said Debra.

"Lori, Ethan and I are all looking forward to seeing you. You know, you're our only family."

Lori looked lovingly at him and gave him a smile.

The next morning his assistant walked into Trent's office.

"Trent, I need to speak with you. Is this a good time?"

"Sure, come in."

Amy closed the door. After she took a seat, she said, "I've heard troubling rumors."

"What kind of rumors?" Trent looked at her searchingly.

"You're going to be fired at tomorrow's board meeting."

"What!" he said as he jerked back. "Who is spreading the rumor?"

"I'm not sure... I think it is Maxell. I heard from one of the admins that Maxell is telling people Hintec's performance has gone from bad to worse. He knows one of the board members very well, and he's convinced that board member you should be fired."

Trent turned grim.

"I shouldn't have bothered you with this," said Amy as she watched his face. "I don't want to spread rumors... I just felt this was serious. I didn't mean to upset you."

"It's all right," he said, with a simmering undertone. "I appreciate you bringing it to me." He looked out the window, lost in thought. "First of all, the company's performance isn't bad," he reassured Amy and himself. "Sales are growing, albeit not as fast as we wanted. Performance wouldn't be a reason to fire me."

He frowned, and she looked at him silently.

"I can't think of a board member who is close to Maxell," he said searching his mind. "This is Maxell making mischief." His faced reddened with anger. "I'm going to teach him a lesson. I can play this game too. Ask Simon to see me right away."

Amy left to call Simon.

When Simon walked in, Trent was standing beside the window looking out.

"What is going on? Is everything okay?" asked Simon.

"Close the door."

Simon closed it and Trent turned to him, his face still red. "Maxell is spreading rumors the board is going to fire me. I'm sick of him. I'm going to fire him."

Before Simon could gather his thoughts, Trent's phone rang. He walked up to it and picked it up.

"Your next appointment is here," said Amy.

"I just need a minute to wrap up with Simon."

He looked at Simon and said, "I wanted to let you know what Maxell was up to. Let's touch base later."

Simon opened the office door and left.

When he reached home that evening, Debra and Ethan were in the game room upstairs. Lori was sitting on the couch in the family room reading a magazine. He bent down and kissed her. He was about to say something when she said, "What is wrong? You have that look."

"It's Maxell," he said, walking to the bay windows and looking out. "He's up to his usual political mischief. I told Simon I'm going to fire Maxell."

"Are you, really?"

Trent turned toward her and shook his head. "No. I just want to spread the rumor. Simon won't be able to keep it to himself, and coming from Simon the rumor will seem authentic."

"Why don't you just fire him?" asked Lori.

He came and sat beside her. "I need to earn the board and Cedric's confidence before I make executive changes. I just want to shake Maxell up a little bit."

"Is that the right thing to do?"

"Oh yeah, it'll be fine. When Maxell gets the message, he'll cool down. After all, he tried to do the same thing to me. This will teach him a lesson. Anyway, did you have your appointment today? What did the doctor say?"

"Yes, after Emily and I picked up Mom, we went to see the doctor. He said I'm past due, and the baby has positioned itself well. I'm to call him as soon as I feel any contractions."

Trent stopped by Amy's cubicle the next morning.

"Lori is close to her delivery. Can you lighten my schedule for the next week?"

"Sure, but before I promise, let me look at your calendar."

Amy looked at Trent's calendar and said, "It's doable. I'll move things over to the following two weeks. You may have to be available for a few conference calls."

"That won't be a problem," he said.

Trent was reviewing his presentation for the board meeting when the phone rang. He answered. It was Lori.

"Honey, my contractions started. They're slow, but the doctor asked me to head over to the hospital. I'm fine, and Mom's driving me. We should be there shortly. Ethan is with Emily."

"I'll come right away," he said standing up.

"No, you have your board meeting. You remember with Ethan I was in labor for twenty hours. Come after the meeting. If anything changes, I'll call you, promise."

Trent put the phone down and sat down. He was gathering his thoughts when Hector barged in. "Are you firing Maxell?"

Trent looked up irritated.

"It's none of your business," said Trent, jabbing his finger at Hector.

"It is my business! I'm a member of the management team," said Hector emphatically. He leaned across the desk, glaring at Trent. "It is my business when you make knee-jerk decisions."

"Excuse me!" roared Trent, as he stood up.

"That's right. Your decisions are terrible. You're a pretty boy with no management experience."

Trent lost his control and shouted loudly, "Forget Maxell. Hector, I am firing you. Right now. YOU ARE FIRED! GET OUT!"

Hector stormed out. Amy rushed in.

He looked at her burning with rage, "Call Oscar and tell him Hector is terminated effective immediately. Ask security to escort him out."

After Amy left, Trent sat down to reflect on all that was happening. Ten minutes before the board meeting, he started gathering his materials for the meeting.

The VP of HR walked in. Before Oscar could say anything, Trent said, "I know why you're here. Let's talk about it after I come back from the board meeting."

Oscar shook his head.

"What is it?" said Trent trying to get his mind to think straight.

"Hector is in the boardroom," said Oscar.

"How can he do that? Who invited him?"

"I'm not sure. Apparently, as he was leaving with his box of personal stuff, he ran into one of the board members, who asked him to join the board meeting."

"I don't believe it! ...Then you come too. I will need your support."

Trent and Oscar headed to the boardroom. Hector was sitting at the table next to John Summers.

John Summers from RiverRock Funds initiated the meeting. "Since Cedric is out of town, I'll lead the meeting today. We have our list of agenda items to go through beginning with the quarterly performance. Trent, why don't you walk us through the numbers?"

"We did better than the first quarter and reached $24 million in new sales. We're moving in the right direction."

"You did $23 million in the first quarter. Sounds to me you are plateauing in new sales. At this rate of new sales, we will shrink this year in total revenues. Isn't that right?" pressed John.

Trent grimaced. "$24 million is a record high for quarterly new sales. Unfortunately, it is just enough to overcome the shortfall due to our low retention rate. We won't shrink this year. I expect we will end up flat in total revenues compared to last year."

"And you're satisfied with that?"

"No, I am not. Of course not," said Trent with a painful look. "Over the last five years, our retention rate has been declining. So far this year, we have prevented further deterioration, but the low retention rate is our biggest problem."

"I'd say," said John in a sarcastic tone. "Do you have a strategy to improve it?"

Trent paused. "We're still looking for a breakthrough."

John shook his head, disgust written on his face, and went through the other agenda items. Then he cleared his throat and said, "We have one more item that needs our attention. Trent, I understand you fired Hector today. Can you explain the reasons behind your decision?"

"I am the CEO, and that decision is mine to make."

"That wasn't the question. What led you to make such a decision and in such a manner — in a fit of rage?"

Trent felt his Blackberry vibrate but didn't answer it.

"Hector is a poor team player," replied Trent. "He has resisted change, poisoned the atmosphere, and consistently questioned my authority."

"Is that right, Oscar?" asked John, looking piercingly at the VP of HR.

"Not completely," replied Oscar calmly. "Hector can be challenging to manage, but his experience is beneficial to Hintec."

Trent's face fell. He felt betrayed.

"Why don't we invite the other management team members so we can hear their views as well," suggested John.

"Why are we creating a referendum?" protested Trent. "This is highly unusual. I haven't seen anything like this in any other company. This isn't a decision that falls under management by committee. This is squarely the CEO's decision."

Trent looked around the room for support. None of the other board members spoke up. He was aghast.

Venkat, Fran and Maxell walked in. As soon as they sat down, John asked for their opinion.

"Hector isn't the easiest person to work with, but we can't afford to lose him," said Fran, matter-of-factly.

"I have a lot of respect for Hector," Venkat said. "He has coached me, and we've worked well together."

John pushed back from the table. "I have heard enough. I ask the board to overrule Trent's decision to fire Hector. When Cedric is back, we can ask him to weigh on this matter. Does the board agree to keep Hector in the role of COO?"

Almost all the board members nodded.

"Good," said John. "This meeting is adjourned."

From the corner of his eye, Trent caught Hector and Maxell's smirk. His face turned red with anger. As the others stood up, Trent got up and walked out of the boardroom.

Back in his office, he sank in his chair, and put his head in his hands, the artery on his forehead throbbing. His Blackberry vibrated. He pulled it out of its holster. Lori's cell phone number flashed on the caller id. He answered.

"Trent, this is Debra. Lori's contractions started progressing quickly once we checked in. I called earlier."

"I was in the meeting. I'll leave right away."

"We're in room 312 in the north wing."

At the hospital, Trent raced frantically through the hallway. He checked the name outside the room and entered. Lori smiled briefly as she saw him but grimaced as the next contraction hit. She had tears in her eyes as she clutched Trent's hand.

The doctor said, "We should have the baby soon."

Lori closed her eyes, and Trent held her hand. Twenty long minutes later, the doctor came in again and encouraged Lori to push harder. Between her gasping for breath and the intense labor pain, Lori was exhausted.

When the baby finally came, Trent kissed Lori's forehead. "Honey, she's beautiful!"

Lori smiled, then slumped back and closed her eyes.

They had agreed to name the baby Catherine when they had learned they were expecting a daughter. While Lori rested, Trent took pictures of Catherine and of Debra holding the baby, looking every bit the proud grandmother.

A few minutes later Lori opened her eyes. Emily walked in with Ethan. Lori encouraged him to give her a hug, but he hesitated. Lori's hair was unkempt and she didn't look her normal self. Trent walked across and put his hand on Ethan's shoulder. "It's Mom, Ethan. You have a new baby sister. Can you say Catherine?"

Debra was staying the night at the hospital. When Trent and Ethan got ready to go home, Trent told Ethan to kiss Lori. As he leaned toward her, Lori caught his hand. She squeezed it and told him she and Catherine would be home soon. Ethan nodded.

Trent drove home with Ethan behind him in his car seat. Ethan was quiet during the trip, and Trent was lost in his thoughts. The incidents since he took over as CEO flashed before his eyes. He felt tired and resigned.

After dinner, Trent sat down on the family room couch to go through his emails on his laptop, but he couldn't get himself to do it. He set his laptop aside, put his feet up on the coffee table, and slumped back into the comfortable leather cushions. Thoughts of work raged through his mind.

Ethan crawled up beside him. At first, Trent hardly noticed him. Finally, he turned to Ethan. As Ethan looked up at his dad, a tear rolled down his cheek. Trent grabbed his son into his lap and hugged him tight against his chest. The father and son were silent. In that large quiet house, the two held onto each other. Soon, they were asleep. The full moon shone brightly through the bay windows from across the placid lake.

When Trent awoke the next morning, he saw Ethan still sleeping on the couch, curled beside him. Trent touched his cheek softly. Then he remembered the previous day's events. As he showered, the events replayed in his head again.

He woke up Ethan and got him ready. After the two ate breakfast, he called his assistant. When she didn't pick up, he remembered it was a Saturday. He called her at home.

"We have a beautiful baby girl," he announced to Amy.

"Congratulations!" said Amy. "How much does she weigh? How's Lori doing?"

"6 pounds, 9 ounces. Lori and Catherine are doing fine. Ethan and I are getting ready to go back to the hospital."

"That's great," said Amy.

"I'll work from home on Monday and Tuesday. Cancel the Monday morning management meeting."

"I didn't get a chance to catch you yesterday before you left. I heard it wasn't a good board meeting. What happened?"

"I don't want to talk about it. I'm tired. I've done everything I know, done my best, but things have only gotten worse. I need to really figure this out… clear my head."

Section 2: Managing Coherently

Chapter in this section:

Chapter 4: Crossroads

Trent and Ethan picked up Lori, Catherine and Debra from the hospital on Sunday.

Once they were home, they settled down. As Catherine slept on the bed, Lori touched her pink cheeks and held her tiny fingers. "I'm relishing this moment with all my family here," said Lori to Trent. He kissed Lori on the forehead.

Ethan ran in, hugged Lori, and ran out. As he watched Ethan run out, Trent recollected, "On Friday night, Ethan had a single tear drop, didn't cry, just that single drop."

"Oh, my baby."

"And, then we hugged," shared Trent. He revealed, "I needed the solace as much as he did."

"Why…," she wondered. Then it hit her, "Wait, what happened at the board meeting?"

Trent looked at her, his face somber.

"What's wrong?" she asked getting anxious.

"We'll talk about it when you recover."

"No. Tell me now what happened."

He recounted Friday's events before and during the board meeting. She kept quiet for a few minutes, reflecting. Then she advised, "Why don't you talk to someone?"

He looked puzzled. "Talk to whom?"

"Someone who can bring another perspective, spark different ideas. You're too close to the situation."

He got up and started pacing slowly. She watched him. He then said, "An outsider couldn't understand my issues. Where would I find someone I was comfortable with?"

"Do something different…. If you keep beating your head against a wall, all you'll get is a bloody head."

He sat down on the chair beside the bed, running his fingers slowly through his hair.

"One way or the other, you need to find a way to resolve the situation," she reinforced.

Trent woke up early Monday morning. Lori was asleep. He took a shower and instead of dressing for the office, put on a t-shirt, shorts, and sneakers. Debra had made coffee. He joined her at the kitchen table.

"Good morning," said Debra, "going somewhere?"

"Jogging," he said.

"How many times did Catherine wake up?" asked Debra.

"Three. Lori took care of her," he said and smiled.

He finished his coffee and left. As he passed the house next-door, he noticed a tall, silver-haired man in the front yard. He waved. "Hi, I'm Trent Wertheimer, your next-door neighbor."

"I'm Watson Hughes," said the man, walking over to shake his hand.

"Yes, I know. My wife had told me a few weeks back that you had moved in. Sorry, I hadn't come by to say hello. I've been very busy and we just had a new baby."

"Well, congratulations!"

"Thanks. Are you new to Houston?" asked Trent.

"We moved from Chicago two years ago."

"What brought you to Houston?" asked Trent engaging in small talk.

"Our daughter, son-in-law, and our two grandkids."

"I hope you'll love this subdivision as much as we do," said Trent looking at the lush landscape and beautiful homes.

"We do. Our daughter bought a house on the next street six months ago. Once we looked at the lake, we decided to move here as well. Come in and have a cup of coffee."

"I just finished a cup," said Trent.

"Would one more hurt?"

Trent joined him. Watson took him to the formal living room, decorated in shades of soft maroon. They sat down on the sofa, and Watson's wife, Martha brought them coffee.

"What do you do?" enquired Trent.

"I'm retired. I serve on the board of a company here in Houston, but it doesn't occupy me much." After taking a sip, he said, "In Chicago, I worked for Globez."

"Sorry, I'm not familiar with them. How big are they?"

"Three billion in revenues with a global footprint."

"What did you do for them?" asked Trent.

"I was the VP of process and performance."

"VP process and performance?"

Watson smiled. "It's an uncommon title; I created mine. I served in that role for 11 years." After taking another sip from the large mug, he continued. "My team acted like internal consultants. Our job was to align the divisions, ensure the strategy was advancing, help measure the right activities and trends, lead change management, and improve processes."

"Quite an important job," said Trent.

"Yes," said Watson reminiscing. "What do you do?"

"I'm CEO of Hintec, a business-intelligence company."

"Very good," said Watson.

They finished the coffee, and as Trent left for the park he said, "Please give my regards to Martha. It was a pleasure to meet you both. And welcome to the neighborhood."

On returning home, Trent went into the master bedroom to see if Lori was up. She was changing Catherine's diaper.

"Mom said you went for a jog," said Lori, looking up.

"Yeah, I did. On the way, I met our new neighbors."

"Martha and Watson?" asked Lori, putting Catherine in her crib.

"Yes, Watson was the VP of process and performance for a large Chicago company."

She looked at him. "What did he do exactly?"

Trent explained. After he finished, she asked, "Is he someone you could talk to."

"How weird would that be? He's a neighbor and I barely know him. If I talk to someone at all, I was thinking it'd be somebody who's been a CEO."

Lori glared at him, as if to tell him not to make excuses.

"Fine. I'll talk to him," he said giving in.

"How can it hurt? You've been struggling, and now, that board meeting is eating you inside. Try him out."

"So am I hiring him as a consultant?" quipped Trent.

"No, just seeking friendly advice, like a sounding board."

"What a quirk of fate? I needed someone to talk to and this man conveniently shows up as my next door neighbor."

"Stop analyzing," chided Lori. "First, see if he's useful."

When Trent rang the bell, Watson opened the door.

"Hi, are you free this evening?" Trent began. "I'd like to invite you to the country club. Normally we'd invite you to our house, but with the baby it's a little challenging."

Watson smiled. "Don't worry about formalities. Why don't you come over here after you finish dinner? Around 6:30? We'll sit on the deck, enjoy the lake, and visit."

"Okay. We'll play host when Catherine's a bit older."

Trent returned home and updated Lori. He then went into his home-office and checked his emails. None made a mention of the board meeting.

He picked up the phone to call his assistant, Amy. He began dialing the numbers, but put the phone down half way through. He got up and for a while stared out at the front yard from the window. Then he sat down, and closed his eyes.

A couple of hours later, Debra walked into the office, "Trent, I have lunch on the table."

"Oh, I'm sorry," he said, startled a little bit. "I've been in the office all this time and forgot to help you with lunch."

"That's not a problem," she said.

Trent cleared the table after lunch. Then he accompanied Lori to the bedroom and helped change Catherine's diaper.

He dialed Amy's number again later in the afternoon. She didn't pick up her phone. He didn't leave a message.

When Trent rang the bell in the evening, the distinguished-looking Watson opened promptly. "Come in," he said. They walked out to the deck. At 6:30 PM, it was still bright. Daylight lasts past 8:30 PM in Houston during summer.

"Thank you. You're very nice," said Trent as they sat down on the patio chairs. "We should have invited you. Instead, here I am enjoying your hospitality and your beautiful deck."

"I'm sure we'll get plenty of opportunities to visit you. How are your wife and baby doing?"

"Quite well. Thanks for asking." Leaning forward Trent said, "I had an ulterior motive to visit with you."

Watson raised an eyebrow, surprised and curious.

"I've been struggling with issues at work," divulged Trent.

Watson smiled. "That's good. The ball gets rolling when an executive realizes he or she needs help."

Trent leaned back with an uncomfortable look on his face. He didn't like the feeling of asking for help. After a pause, he said, "I just need a sounding board."

"I'll be happy to be a sounding board," Watson reassured. "I love thinking and talking about business and office issues. What's on your mind? What's bothering you?"

Trent recounted the events since he became CEO. It took a while. Finally, he said, "I'm overwhelmed with all the issues." He looked at his watch. "Wow, I've completely lost sense of time. You're a great listener."

"You're welcome to continue."

"No, I've taken up a lot of your time this evening, and Lori will be waiting. I'm working from home tomorrow. If you're willing we could meet tomorrow."

"Sure. We could meet at 9:00 AM if that works for you. I have some questions and feedback."

"How did it go?" asked Lori. She was resting on the couch while Debra was rocking Catherine in the bedroom.

He sat down. "I was hesitant but Watson put me at ease. It allowed me to open up. I feel as if a weight's been lifted."

She stretched her arms and hugged him.

Trent called Amy the next morning. She answered.

"How're things going?" he asked.

"It's been quiet."

"You mean?"

"No one said anything to me yesterday about the board meeting or what happened. It could be that everyone's busy or it could be that no one's telling me...."

"Hmm...," reflected Trent.

"I can dig around," she offered.

"If you hear something, let me know."

"I will. How's everything with Lori and Catherine?"

"They're doing great. Lori's recovering well."

Trent put down the phone, and left to see Watson.

Clad in khakis and a tee shirt, Watson opened the door. "Come in. Are you getting enough sleep?"

"Yes. Catherine wakes up, but it's not been bad."

"And, how's Catherine doing?"

"She's doing great. I love her." Trent smiled. "She's cute. You and Martha should come over."

"We'd love to. I'll tell Martha. Where will you be most comfortable, here in the living room or out on the deck?"

"I like your deck. Let's go out there."

Watson led the way to the oak stained deck. They sat under the shade of the balcony. The cool morning breeze rippled across the lake.

"I want to understand you better... so I'll probe and push," said Watson, setting the stage.

"Please, go ahead."

"Were you the best candidate to be Hintec's CEO?"

"Absolutely. Hintec wasn't growing. After I came in as VP sales, I closed big deals and gave the company a new life."

"How did that make you a good candidate for CEO?"

"Sales are what drive any company. I was the best candidate to be CEO as I would be able to drive sales higher."

Watson leaned forward, a serious expression on his face. "Do you see a difference between the VP sales and the CEO role?"

Trent became quiet. "As VP sales, I cared less about marketing or engineering." Closing his eyes for a second, he said, "Being CEO is a lot harder. Now I have to make all the pieces work together."

"Have you had any experience in other functional areas: marketing, engineering, customer service?"

"No. Why do you ask?"

"Working in different roles could have accorded you a broader perspective. When executives come with only one functional experience, their answers tend to be limited, reflecting only that area."

"I can see that. When Barry took over as CEO, being a software engineer, he focused heavily on the software," said Trent, not making the connection to himself.

"You had a sales background, and therefore your initiatives had a heavier sales growth focus." Watson looked down at the deck, rubbing his chin.

"I don't understand where you're headed with your questions," said Trent perplexed and dissatisfied. "I need help dealing with my current situation, not an analysis of my experience and background."

Watson looked up. "Your current situation is a symptom. We'll address it, but first we must understand the root cause of your problems."

"What is the root cause of my problems?"

Watson looked into Trent's eyes. "As CEO, you should've done a much better job."

Trent's face fell. "Why?" he said, struggling a little bit.

"You mean…," Watson, began to say.

Trent finished the sentence, "Yes. Why do you think I did a poor job?"

Continuing to look intently at him, Watson said, "Before we understand that, you must do something."

"What's that?" said Trent, not sure, he liked the conversation.

"Take your emotions out of this conversation. Separate yourself from the situation and look at it objectively. Then you won't fall in the ego-trap."

Trent was irritated. "In your assessment, what didn't I do right?"

Watson sighed. "I don't see you following a systematic approach. There's little clarity and coherence in your actions and decisions."

Trent stared out at the lake.

Watson said gently, "Let's understand well a business leader's role. Once we do that, you'll have an opportunity to remedy your situation."

Watson waited while Trent thought.

Trent finally spoke. Explaining his approach, he said, "I was doing all the right things, attacking the issues and pushing people to get things done. It seemed coherent to me. What should I have done differently?"

Watson smiled as if he had seen a light at the end of the tunnel, "That's the million-dollar question. I bet you've asked that in the past, but now you're asking it in earnest."

"What should I have done differently? What should I still do differently?" murmured Trent, looking down and moving his eyes from side to side, searching for answers.

Watson answered, "As you know, a business is complex, involving numerous variables: economy, markets, competition, internal process and product capabilities, people, office politics, change, and evolution."

"Yes," agreed Trent as he looked up.

"The interaction of these variables creates a smorgasbord of choices. On top of that, everyone has a different interpretation of what's important, and different expectations from the company and from each other."

"You're telling me. Everyone has their own opinion."

Watson interlocked his fingers. "You must make sense of all these variables and choices for Hintec. Once you use a well-described, systematic method, people will see the logical flow. They'll understand what they need to do and how it all fits. The clearer you make things, the more power you'll unleash within your organization. Successful companies have two common traits — clarity and coherence."

Trent got up from his chair, walked over and leaned against the deck's railing. "I've tried to do just that," he protested. "I thought you were going to reveal something profound. This is common sense. Everyone knows it."

Watson smiled. Pointing at Trent, he said, "You know it... but you haven't done it. And, you don't really understand it."

Trent looked at Watson with quizzing eyes. "What do you mean I don't understand it? I've been working for twenty years in sales and management."

"Let's understand the point here. In baseball, you have amateur and professional players. Both play with the same rules, but the professionals play the game at a much higher level of performance. You've performed your CEO duties at an amateur level not a professional level."

Trent's face flashed red.

"I see you need time to reflect," observed Watson.

Trent was about to comment when Martha walked in. "Our daughter and grandkids are here," she shared. "They've come over for lunch." Looking at Trent, she said, "Are you okay? You look red."

"It's just the heat," replied Trent. "I should head back home," he said standing up.

"We'd love to come over and see the baby," said Martha.

"Sure, we'd like that."

"Ask your wife, if this evening is convenient."

"I'll call you back and let you know."

Trent politely thanked Watson and headed home.

When he returned home, Lori was setting up the table. "Mom went to pick up Ethan from the daycare," shared Lori. "We can eat as soon as they're back." He helped her.

Then they walked to the family room. She sat down on the couch and moved the cushion to her side. He sat down beside her. "Watson told me I performed poorly as a CEO." He frowned. "I think he called me an amateur CEO."

She laughed out aloud. He looked at her aghast at first, and then smiled. She rubbed his shoulder. "Honey, it's okay.

He's challenging your thinking and perspective so you can drop your shield. Unless you do, he can't help you."

He shook his head. "I needed a sounding board, not a beat-the-crap-out-of-me board." He looked at his watch. "I have a conference call with a customer, and I need to touch base with Simon about a couple of proposals, and also call Amy. Oh, and, Martha asked if they could come by this evening. Could you call her?"

"I will," said Lori.

After lunch, Trent retreated to his home-office. He checked his voice mail and emails, and then dialed Amy at work. She answered.

"How's everything? Did anyone ask about me?"

"No one's asked. They know you're taking care of your wife and baby...."

"Is something wrong?" He could sense her reticence.

"I don't want to bother you," she said hesitating.

"No, tell me," he pressed.

"Someone asked me if you were going to continue as CEO."

Trent drooped and his face tightened as he remembered he would have to face the Chairman. "Is Cedric in," he asked.

"I understand he's flying back from his trip on Thursday. He's expected to be in the office on Monday."

"Would you set up time for me to see him on Monday?"

"Sure. Are you coming in tomorrow?"

"Yes."

"I moved your meetings, so nothing requires your physical presence in the office over the next three days. You should work from home; it'll be a good break," suggested Amy, knowing he could use the time away from the office.

"I'll see," said Trent.

Martha and Watson arrived in the evening. After introductions, Lori looked at Watson and said. "I've heard a lot about you."

"And you're still happy to see me," joked Watson.

"Absolutely, thank you so much for being a sounding board. Trent tells me you're asking challenging questions."

Watson smiled, knowing very well that Trent didn't appreciate his assessment.

"Where's that precious baby?" Martha interrupted.

"Asleep," said Trent and led the way into the bedroom.

"She's beautiful," Martha whispered and Watson nodded.

They returned to the living room and visited for a while, until Martha stood up, "We better get going. Lori needs her rest," she said, smiling. "When Catherine is old enough to be out, you must bring her over to see us."

As they were leaving, Watson turned to Trent and asked, "Do you want to meet again tomorrow morning?"

"I had planned to go to the office." He paused, and then said, "I'll come over in the morning."

Lori smiled. "I'm happy to see Trent engaged with you."

Watson nodded and smiled.

After Watson and Martha left, Trent said, "I didn't realize you liked Watson so much."

"I like that he's helping you."

Trent shook his head. He later sent Amy an email saying he wasn't going to come into the office the next day.

In the morning, Trent called Amy. She answered.

"Cedric called. He's back in town," she told him. "I've set up your meeting with him on Monday morning."

"Did he ask for me?"

"Yes, I told him you were at an appointment this morning. He said he'll talk to you on Monday when he'll be in the office."

Trent's face turned dour.

"Remember, you have a conference call at 3:00 PM today with the president of the business-intelligence conference."

"I remember. Thanks."

He got up, went to the kitchen and told Lori, "I'm going to see Watson," and left.

"Come in. Can I get you some coffee?" asked Watson.

"No, thanks, I just had breakfast."

Watson grabbed coffee for himself and they headed out.

The air was cooler as it had rained overnight. Watson took a beach towel and wiped dry two chairs.

"I have a question for you," said Trent sitting down.

"Sure, shoot."

"I feel you've been critical of me. I didn't come to you to be judged. Why?"

Watson put his large coffee mug on the patio table. "You've asked for my help, but before I can help you, I've to shake you out of your complacence and resistance. You have to accept your responsibility in precipitating the situation."

Trent was silent.

After pausing for a moment, Watson said, "Do you know what makes an alcoholic turn the corner? It's when he or she says I have a problem. Likewise, I can help an executive only when he or she says I have a problem and means it."

Trent remained quiet. Watson was about to continue when Trent spoke, his voice quivering, "I went through hell in that board meeting, Hector's smirk haunts me day and night."

Watson closed his eyes briefly.

Trent stared down. "I know I need help. Lori is right; I need to learn how to deal with these types of situations."

Watson leaned forward and touched his arm. "I can help you. I've worked with hundreds of executives, I've seen a lot."

"Have you been through a situation like mine?"

"Yes. But I must set your expectations. I have no silver bullet, no magic answer to solve your problems in fifteen minutes. Everything I share is common sense. There's no earth shattering idea here. But, stick with me and you'll realize how all the seemingly simple things come together to make a powerful difference."

Trent looked at Watson, waiting for him to continue.

"As we discussed yesterday, you must follow a systematic method," reiterated Watson. "And, why is being systematic so important? The best rocket scientists, lawyers, surgeons, stock investors and the best leaders are systematic. They don't wing it. They don't achieve success by accident, coincidence, a stroke of luck, or by shooting from their hips."

Trent nodded to acknowledge Watson's point.

"What would happen to the best athlete in the world, if he or she isn't focused or doesn't follow their well-practiced routine on the day of the Olympics?"

"They'll lose."

"Exactly. The best professionals are systematic. That doesn't mean they're not spontaneous and agile. They are, but they're always aware of the big picture."

Watson took a deep breath, and looked at Trent. "So are you ready to receive help Mr. Wertheimer? You're at the crossroads and must decide if you're ready to turn over a new leaf."

Trent pressed his palms together. "I understand what you're saying. I'm ready to do it. More importantly, do it seriously."

"I'm pleased to hear that."

"I recognize the value of a systematic method, but how will it help me with my current situation, and how could it have prevented the situation."

"Great question," said Watson in a reassuring tone. "Think about it. The loss of your key customers, the differences you have with Venkat and Hector, the challenges with Maxell, the lack of clear guidelines for the customer service team, the pushing through of staff reduction, are all examples of events and actions that reflect a discordant approach."

"I see that, now," admitted Trent to Watson, and perhaps for the first time to himself.

"I have developed a systematic and coherent management method, but you're welcome to use any management method you like. The specific method is not half as important as being systematic and coherent in your thinking and actions. There are many ways to skin a cat."

"I haven't used an organized management method. It's really been a combination of things that made sense to me. I do want to learn your method."

"Okay," said Watson encouraged. "As we discuss the method, we'll take many of your actions and events, and evaluate them against the backdrop of the method. That will provide you the context to judge which are the right decisions and actions."

"That'll be helpful. It'll make things clearer for me."

Trent returned home and went into his home-office. Lori came in as he was writing down some notes. "You look calm," she said. "How was your meeting?"

"It was good."

"And...," she probed.

"I understand where Watson's coming from. I asked him what I should do differently. He didn't answer with a new management fad."

"What did he say?"

"Use a systematic method to drive clarity and coherence. That resonates with me. I've been reacting to issues. I haven't connected things." He sighed.

"You seem to be on the right track," she said, pleased with his demeanor.

Trent closed his eyes for a second. "I wonder if I'll be able to redeem myself. Can I use Watson's method and wisdom to put the company back on track? And, how should I change personally?"

"I'm stunned," said Lori. "I've always seen you on the move. For the first time, I see you reflective and self-aware." As she poked him in the side, she said, "You must be maturing."

Trent's Notes

Management and Leadership Takeaways

1. Successful companies have two common traits — clarity and coherence. The differing preferences, expectations and interpretations about what drives the business can make an organization inefficient and ineffective. A business leader must work relentlessly at ensuring clarity and coherence in the organization.

2. The best rocket scientists, lawyers, surgeons and stock investors are systematic. You cannot run a business based on instinct alone. A leader must use a systematic method to connect all the strategic elements in the business, so everyone can see the logical flow.

3. A business leader must appreciate and value all aspects of the business, not just the area of his/her functional expertise and preference. Otherwise, his/her organization will develop a skewed focus.

Personal Takeaways

1. You must be willing to accept responsibility for your actions and thinking, and be open to changing yourself.

Chapter 5: Cohegic Method

"What a beautiful morning," said Watson as he and Trent walked out to the deck the next day.

"Crisp and bright," agreed Trent. "I'm eager to learn your systematic method," he said, sitting down.

"Let's get right into it. I call it the Cohegic Method," said Watson waving his hands in a grand gesture.

Trent smiled at his enthusiasm, and asked, "Cohegic?"

"Is a made-up word. I derived it from strategic coherence — tying together of all the important elements for managing an enterprise." Watson took out a sheet (Figure 1) from his portfolio. "I have a diagram for you."

Trent took the sheet and placed it on the coffee table.

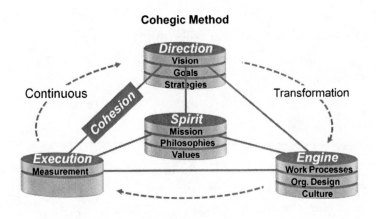

Figure 1

Watson pointed to the diagram and said, "Cohegic has five facets. If you look at any organization logically and holistically, whether it is a Fortune 500 corporation or a one-person business, you will see five facets: spirit, direction, engine, execution, and cohesion. As you understand each facet, you will come across key questions. Answering those questions will be an eye-opening experience for you and your team. It will for sure, clarify your issues and provide a path for your team to be on the same page."

"I'd love for that to happen," said Trent as he studied the diagram.

"As you can see, at the center is the static facet spirit. The corners are the dynamic facets: direction, engine, and execution. The bars tying the whole structure together is cohesion, keeping the dynamic facets in-sync."

"And, you cycle through the three dynamic facets," said Trent as he traced his finger around the circle.

"Yes, in each cycle you would increase your understanding, challenge previous assumptions, reinvent, rebuild, and redeliver. If done right, Hintec's strategies, capabilities, and execution will improve with each cycle. As long as Hintec is in business, it must cycle and transform continuously."

"Can we go through an overview of the five facets?" asked Trent.

"Of course. Let's start with spirit. It defines what the organization is about, its DNA, its passion, and its reason for existence. Once crystallized, spirit is static. It's the soul of the organization. Spirit has three components: mission, core philosophies, and values. At Hintec, you have many problems because your spirit isn't crystallized."

"Our spirit isn't crystallized?" said Trent with a puzzled look.

"We'll dive deeper into that later."

"All right," said Trent. He took out his pocket tablet and made a note, "Crystallize spirit."

When he finished writing, Watson said, "The next facet, direction is about deliberating on the right course, validating the choices based on execution data, and adjusting the course accordingly. Vision, goals, and strategies are part of direction. You must succinctly articulate the direction."

"Have I articulated Hintec's direction well?"

"You've got room for improvement."

"Okay," said Trent thoughtfully.

Watson pointed to the engine disk on the diagram and said, "Just as an engine powers the sports car you drive, every organization has an engine that provides the underpinnings on which it operates and accomplishes its vision and strategies. The components of the engine facet are work processes, organizational design, and culture."

"I shouldn't even ask your views on our engine," said Trent as he shook his head. "I know our culture is broken, and given our customer service challenges, our work processes need help. I wonder how we'll fix it all."

"How do you create an ocean?"

Trent looked puzzled.

"One drop at a time. It'll take a lot of effort, but with all these drops of effort we'll create the Hintec Ocean."

Trent smiled.

"Do I amuse you," asked Watson.

Trent laughed.

Clapping his hands, Watson said, "And, now, execution, the actions Hintec will take to achieve its direction."

Trent looked down. "Execution has been my mantra, and yet I've executed poorly."

"I've seen it often," said Watson. "Organizations have great ideas, but the execution of those ideas is often lacking. The implementation is often as bad as the ideas are good."

"I know what you're saying. Often things don't turn out as well as the original idea," lamented Trent.

"And now," Watson said, lowering his voice for effect, "the most overlooked facet of all."

"Cohesion?"

"Yes," said Watson, nodding vigorously. "Direction, engine, and execution must move in harmony with each other and with spirit. Even one facet being out-of-sync leads to ambiguity, destroys focus, and skews alignment."

"And leads to poor performance," added Trent.

"Exactly." Spreading his fingers to illustrate, Watson said, "These five facets are the pillars of business performance. Understanding the five facets and ensuring cohegic flow is your path to helping Hintec perform at its maximum level. Address them, and you'll find the answers to resolve your issues."

Trent looked at Watson quizzically.

Watson slapped his knee and stood up. "That's it. That's the method."

Trent took a second look at the diagram. "I think I've done most of what you cover here."

"You've implemented quick fixes piecemeal," said Watson reminding Trent of his modus operandi.

"I recognize that. But what's new here?" said Trent, unimpressed with what he had heard so far.

"This method will provide context and clarity, first in our discussions and then in your actions at Hintec," said Watson trying to get Trent to appreciate the need for the method.

Trent fidgeted not willing to buy Watson's pitch. Watson sat down beside him.

"To solve your problems you need a work-style change, not another quick fix."

"I realize that completely," said Trent. "And this method will do it?" he asked seeking an assurance.

"Absolutely. On the surface, the method seems simple, as it should. But as we discuss it in details, you'll realize you don't understand each facet, nor the interaction of the facets as a system, as well as you should. The challenge and opportunity as you know is always in the details."

"Ain't that the truth? I'll give it a try."

"Do you mean it? I don't want a half-hearted attempt," said Watson testing Trent.

"I mean it. I do want a work-style change," said Trent, serious in his determination.

"Okay, good."

Martha stepped onto the deck with two glasses of cold water. "It's hot, why don't you sit inside," she suggested.

They drank the water and retreated to Watson's home-office, sitting at the round mahogany table.

Trent put the Cohegic diagram on the table. "Why do you call the cycles, transformation? It sounds daunting."

Watson explained, "Animal and plant species continuously transform, evolving to adapt to the ever-changing environment. It's the same in business, transform continuously, or become extinct. Some companies misconstrue growth and improvement as doing more of the same. Transformation calls for a fundamental rewiring of every dynamic facet of your business over and over again as the company evolves."

"So you see transformation as ongoing and peaceful. Not revolutionary but evolutionary," observed Trent.

"Revolution is necessary at times, but I consider evolution to be more powerful."

Trent reflected on the conversation and made some notes.

Watson looked at his watch and stood up. "It's almost lunch time. Let's break and resume in the afternoon if your schedule permits. You're welcome to join us for lunch."

"No, thanks. I'll have lunch with the family. Can we meet in the evening? I have two conference calls this afternoon."

"Evening works well for me."

Debra had made chicken casserole. Taking a second helping, Trent told her, "I'm going to miss your cooking."

"Are you saying I don't cook well," teased Lori, giving him a dirty look. "How was your meeting?"

They heard Catherine cry in the bedroom.

"I'll go," offered Debra.

"Thanks, Mom," said Lori.

"Watson is describing his method, which connects all aspects of the organization," said Trent. "When I pushed changes in Hintec, I saw them as one-time initiatives. I need to think of improvements on a continuum."

"That makes sense," said Lori.

That evening, after they sat down, Watson began. "We've discussed the Cohegic method as a vital tool for improving a business. Now, for the tough part."

Trent wondered what was coming next. Looking Trent directly in the eyes, Watson said, "Business transformation without personal transformation is unsustainable."

Trent raised his brow.

"You could develop all the goals and strategies, but if people don't see you act maturely, they won't take you seriously. Of course, you could be a mature leader, but unless you stick to a systematic method…,"

"So, you need both, personal and business transformation."

"That's right. As part of your personal transformation, let's talk about what I call the Alexander complex."

"The Greek king?" asked Trent, bemused.

"Yes. Alexander believed he had God-like powers. His courage and confidence were contagious and his armies won battles even when the odds were against them."

"That's why they call him Alexander the Great," said Trent.

"But that very sense of invincibility led to his downfall. In a battle, he charged ahead leaving the cover of his army behind. Shot at a close range by an arrow, he suffered a fatal wound."

"That's true," said Trent, again not making the connection to himself.

Watson looked again directly into Trent's eyes. "We all have a little bit of the Alexander complex in us. You must be self-aware so you don't drink your own Kool-Aid. Protect Hintec from your shortcomings."

"How?"

"Hiring people smarter and different than you is one way."

Trent winced. "My problem is I have people who challenge me all the time. I won't be a weak nincompoop stuck in a gridlock trying to build consensus."

"I'm not advocating weak leadership."

"Then what are you saying?" Trent narrowed his eyes.

"Don't let your brilliance prevent you from listening. Even the smartest person can't have the best ideas all the time. Carl Sagan, a renowned scientist often said intellectual brilliance is no guarantee against being dead wrong."

"If a leader shouldn't push his ideas, what's his job? Is he a glorified consensus builder? A gopher between all the parties?"

Watson leaned forward. "The leader has an extremely important function to perform."

Trent sat up straight. "What's that?"

"Provide focus!" asserted Watson. "Focus," he repeated. "After listening to all the ideas, the leader must set the agenda. Without a clear decision, the multitude of opinions will make the organization dysfunctional. Clarity and focus are your biggest contribution as a leader."

Trent thought about it. It made sense to him. He made some notes and they concluded the meeting.

"Watson says I must change," Trent told Lori. "He says personal transformation is as important as business transformation."

They were in the kitchen. She was packing a snack for Ethan to take the next day to daycare. "I agree with that," she said.

Trent narrowed his eyebrows.

"I'm not saying you need a personal transformation," she said, snapping the snack bag shut as she looked at him with a straight face and then broke into a smile.

"Yeah, right," he said. Looking at the completed snack bag and then at her, he added, "By the way, isn't tomorrow Saturday. Why are you packing a snack for Ethan?"

"Ah…," she slapped herself on the forehead.

"Who's the one in need of a transformation now?" he said and laughed, only to get a big frown from her.

Trent was in and out all day Saturday running errands. After dinner, as he was getting ready to leave for his evening meeting with Watson, Ethan said, "Daddy, play with me."

"Buddy, I've got to go."

When Ethan insisted, Trent took a few minutes to roll Ethan's favorite red ball to him before he left.

"I have a question," said Trent as he and Watson walked out to the deck to enjoy the cool of the evening. From the corner of his eye, Trent saw a snowy egret, a bird that looks like a small white crane catch a fish. Both men turned to look as the bird flew away with the fish held between its beaks.

"What's your question," asked Watson, as they sat down.

In a low voice, Trent said, "I go back to the office Monday. Everyone will know… how I was humiliated. I appreciate the method and the personal transformation, but I still have a crisis, a fire burning."

"What should you do in case of fire?"

"Run!"

Watson laughed. "What if you can't run away?"

"Cut the supply of oxygen, cut access to the fuel."

"In this context, what's the fuel, what's the oxygen?"

Trent thought for a moment. "Hector, Maxell, me… are all contributing to the fire."

"What should you do? Can you change Maxell and Hector?"

"No."

"Can you change yourself?"

"Yes… maybe," said Trent searching himself.

"How can you change yourself?" nudged Watson.

"I don't know. That's where I need help," said Trent looking at Watson.

"Was your decision to fire Hector wise?"

"It was a good decision for the company, but I did it wrong."

"Because you became emotional, you lost control. Can you overlook your loss of face and do the right thing?"

"What's the right thing?" Without waiting for an answer, Trent said, "Of course… mea culpa. Own up to my mistake."

"Let's make sure we understand what your mistake was. Wasn't your response justified? Maxell spread the rumor, and Hector barged in, defending him."

"Maxell made mischief, but my mistake was falling for it. I reacted to both Maxell and Hector and let my emotions take control."

"Didn't Maxell deserved to be taught a lesson, didn't he?"

"You're right, he did. I… we needed to channel Maxell. I could have let Oscar, my VP of HR, deal with it. My insecurity about being fired, plus my anger and distaste for Maxell led me to lash out."

Satisfied with Trent's answers, Watson said, "Your ability to view your actions dispassionately will allow you to realize what you're doing and if it's appropriate. Great political leaders routinely ask themselves how history will judge them."

Trent nodded.

"Your attitude, behavior, and actions set the stage for the culture of Hintec. You could serve as the best example by explaining and correcting your mistake."

Watson pressed, "Can you do it?"

"I will," said Trent, conviction in his voice.

The family room and the kitchen were dark when Trent reached home. Lori was in bed reading her book. Catherine lay sleeping.

"How did it go," Lori asked.

"Fine," he replied. "I'm sleepy."

He changed his clothes and got into bed. She snuggled up to him. He turned and put his arm around her.

The next morning, as they had coffee, Lori asked, "Are you ready to go back to the office tomorrow?" They were alone. Debra was playing with Ethan in the backyard.

"Uh...," he murmured and shrugged his shoulders, "I guess." Not wanting to discuss any further, he got up and walked outside to join Debra and Ethan.

"You haven't said much all day," said Lori, as they retired for the night. "Are you doing okay?"

"Yes," he replied and walked into his large, well-organized closet and picked out a starched white shirt and a dark suit. He took down a bright tie that was his favorite, looked at it, and then returning it to the rack, selected a conservative red silk tie.

Early Monday morning, Trent met with the Chairman. He recounted the events, and sincerely expressed his regrets.

Cedric stared at him silently and then said, "I'm under quite a bit of pressure because of you. If it weren't for me, the board would've had your head."

Trent felt terrible. He knew how much pressure Cedric would've faced. He nodded his head slowly. "I appreciate your support. I've found an advisor," he shared.

"Well," said Cedric as he rose to leave, "You seem a changed man. I'm glad you have an advisor and I'm pleased with your demeanor. But you have a long way to go. I would work very hard before the next board meeting. Their confidence has been shaken."

Trent felt the weight of a mountain on his shoulders.

When Trent walked into the conference room for the Monday morning meeting, the team was already there. As he entered, a hush fell over the room.

Even though the chair at the head of the table was unoccupied, he sat in an empty chair along one side. "Amy told me some of you called to ask if this meeting was still on. Yes, it is on and… I will continue to lead Hintec."

He looked around. There was little reaction.

"I'm sure everyone knows what happened at the board meeting. I won't rehash what happened and why." He looked down at the table, and in a low voice added, "I've realized I need to change." He could hear his breathing. The whole situation seemed surreal, as if things were moving in slow motion.

When he looked up, he saw their faces, eyes looking at him, ears listening to every word. Coming out of his trance, he said, "I've been managing from my gut. That might be appropriate at times, but it can't be my predominant manner in leading."

Slowly unfurling his hand, he continued, "How will I lead from now on?" He closed his eyes. The room remained silent, waiting. "In a coherent manner where it's clearer what I... what we're thinking, how it all connects and where our focus is. We've to answer three questions to perform better. How do we become more coherent in our thinking and actions? How do we mitigate politics and build the right culture? How do we tie it all together from mission to execution?"

There was shifting around the table, but everyone listened as if their ears had grown an inch taller.

"I've made mistakes and I must improve. I have an advisor now who's helping me change my personal approach and teach me a coherent method to lead and manage Hintec."

He waited for a moment. "Any questions?" he asked.

Oscar, the VP of HR, spoke, to cut the silence. "Who's the advisor?"

"Watson Hughes, a retired corporate executive. He's highly experienced, and has worked with hundreds of executives. I've developed a good deal of faith in his advice. I'll keep you posted on how that develops and share the advice he shares with me." Looking around, he asked, "Any other questions?"

Since no one else spoke, he ended the meeting.

An hour later, his assistant walked into his office. Trent looked up.

"Everyone was pleasantly surprised in today's meeting," Amy said after she sat down. "I hear you spoke deliberately, and while you were conciliatory, you were confident. Folks said this is the first time they've heard you admit a mistake."

Trent listened but offered no response.

"It's good to have you back. I hope you're all right," said Amy, trying to look into his eyes. "You seem to be on another planet. Please let me know if I can help."

"I will. Thanks for your support."

In the afternoon, the VP of HR came by. He closed the door, and Trent invited him to sit down.

"As leaders sometimes we wrongly believe we must have a strong front all the time," said Oscar. "Today, you demonstrated vulnerability, an openness to be wrong. You were no longer the Trent who always insisted on driving his point of view."

Trent smiled briefly. "Thanks, Oscar. I appreciate your feedback. Let's see how the future unfolds."

"You're back at a normal hour. That's unusual," said Lori when he reached home that evening.

"I want to go see Watson after dinner."

"How did things go?" she asked. He quickly reviewed the day for her, and after dinner, left to see Watson.

"Thank you Watson, your advice helped me today," Trent said as soon as Watson opened the door. "I had feared the worst, and last week I didn't think I could even go back. Amy and Oscar told me I have a different perspective now."

"That's good," approved Watson as they walked out.

"Even Cedric said I was a changed man... but he made it clear I must regain the board's confidence. I may have only until the next board meeting to do that," said Trent, his face tense.

"If you resist the temptation for band-aid solutions and adopt a logical and coherent approach, the board's confidence will be a natural by-product. Make Hintec cohegic."

"Absolutely," Trent said.

After they sat down, Trent said, "Last night I thought I had changed and become a new me. Now I feel differently... I'm not a saint."

"What do you mean?"

"I made a mistake, but so did Maxell and Hector. At the risk of you chastising me, I'm still quite angry at them."

"I appreciate your candidness. Last night you had apprehensions about going back. It put you in a reflective mood. Now the pressure has released and your thinking is reverting. All of us make promises to think and act better, and then we revert."

Trent gazed at the lake. "Making it stick is the challenge."

"It's a long journey. Let's dissect your anger. Tell me, in general what makes you angry?"

"I don't want to go through psychoanalysis," said Trent brushing off Watson. "We haven't sufficiently addressed Maxell and Hector. I can talk to them all day long but I won't get anywhere. I need to take some action."

Watson became stern. "I'm not going to do that!"

"Do what?" Trent asked, surprised and annoyed.

"I'm not going to endorse vindictive actions," said Watson firmly.

Neither man said anything. Watson stood up.

Trent broke the impasse. "I'm angry... very angry."

Watson watched him, and then said, "I can appreciate your anger. The gut-wrenching loss of face is hounding you. But you must break the cycle. If your emotions remain in control, as they are at this moment, you'll make another mistake. I wish I could reach into your heart and comfort you."

Trent was breathing heavily.

"This is your test. Two weeks ago, you didn't know any better. Now you do. This is a litmus test for you and me. I'm going to watch closely to see if I can help you or not."

Watson sat down. "You have to understand the cause of your anger to be able to control it."

Watson excused himself and brought Trent a glass of cold water.

"You're in pain and that pains me," said Watson putting his hand on Trent's shoulder. "I'm not an anger management expert, but I hope we can take the sting out of your anger." He sat down.

Trent nodded without making eye contact.

"You have high expectations of yourself and others. When others don't live up to your expectations, you get upset."

Trent nodded again.

"People around you are neither as smart nor as fast as you. You have little tolerance when they don't get what you're saying or work at your pace."

"That's right," mumbled Trent.

"Because you lack the patience and the tolerance, you resort to anger. If you learn to control your anger, you'll be more effective." Tapping his forehead, Watson said, "Anger signifies our lack of control. It's difficult to tell our mind not to be angry — it won't listen. We need other mechanisms to calm it."

"What mechanisms?"

"I'll share an exercise that helps me stay calm. Every night I take fifteen minutes to sit, without any distractions, in a recliner to allow my mind to breathe, and think through the day's events."

"What will happen if I do this?"

"A clear mind will help you make better decisions the next day. You'll begin to see what you could've done differently, what you didn't get a chance to do. After a few weeks of regular practice, you'll notice a change in yourself, you'll be calmer."

"Playing golf calms me and so does jogging."

"Activities such as golfing, exercising, watching TV and sleeping keep your mind either occupied or turned off, they don't allow your mind to unwind."

"What if it doesn't work or I don't like doing it?"

"Try it before you judge."

"Okay," conceded Trent.

"Now that you're calmer, tell me, what was Maxell and Hector's mistake?"

"Maxell spread the rumor. He disrupted Hintec's focus and workings. Hector was disrespectful."

"Hector expressed his opinion in private to you. He wasn't being subversive; he was being judgmental and insolent. Much as you dislike him, all he seems to be doing is standing up for others. Reach out and see if you can mend your relationship."

Trent didn't like the suggestion.

"Maxell on the other hand was subversive and corrupting the culture. He needs a warning and possibly disciplinary action. Of course, first ascertain if Maxell did spread those rumors."

"Okay," said Trent.

"You formed a low opinion of Barry, Hector and Maxell, and as a result have missed the ways they could have helped you."

"I hope you realize how hard it is to, as you say, work with them," said Trent. "Many CEOs say their biggest mistake was not firing the wrong person soon enough."

"In an ideal world, you'd have all the right people who match your intelligence and temperament. In the real world, you might not have a choice. Employees, you may replace, but you also have to deal with vendors, customers, and investors."

"That's a valid point."

"Learning to deal with people is a critical skill. Your frenzy strains your relationships."

Watson stretched his arms above his head. "Let's tie our discussion back to the five facets and categorize the issues."

"That should be interesting."

"The issue of anger pertains to your behavior, which falls under culture, a component of engine."

"Of course."

"The issue of Maxell has evolved into a behavior and hence a culture issue, but originally, it was a direction issue. Maxell and you had different expectations regarding marketing. A common agreement on the marketing goals may have resulted in a better relationship. So this issue falls under direction."

"I tried to get Maxell on the same page. I guess I should've tired harder."

"At the surface, Hector is a culture issue, but below the surface, it's a role and responsibilities issue. What's the description of the ideal candidate for the COO role and the VP customer service role? How well does Hector fit those roles? Approaching it from that angle may provide you an objective assessment. Hence, this issue falls under organizational design, a component of engine."

"I'm beginning to get some sense for this."

"Correctly categorizing each issue under the right facet can give you a better handle on solving them."

"Hopefully, I can solve all the issues."

Watson wagged his finger. "The goal isn't just to solve the issues, but to reduce the number of issues that arise. From the moment you became CEO, you've been caught in the weeds — the issues and the politics. You haven't raised the level of discussion. As a leader, it's up to you to set the right context."

Trent narrowed his forehead in thought. "I'm not sure, I follow."

Watson pulled out a blank sheet of paper and drew a line on it about two inches long. Handing Trent the pen he asked, "How can you make this line seem shorter without re-drawing it or erasing it?"

Trent drew a second line six inches long.

"If the shorter line represents the issues, the longer line represents the new context," said Watson. "It's difficult to make the never-ending list of issues seem smaller unless you create a larger context that reorients everyone to look up and not down."

"Create a larger context," Trent mused staring at the lines.

"Yes. Create an exciting vision that focuses everyone on the future."

"That's easier said than done," pushed back Trent.

"Of course, but you have no choice. That will be the real test of your leadership abilities."

"How was the session?" asked Lori.

"Good."

"Is that it?" she pressed.

"I've a lot to improve; a lot to do. It's a big challenge. As I was walking home, a line from Robert Frost's poem played in my mind — I have miles to go before I sleep."

Trent's Notes

Management and Leadership Takeaways

1. A leader does not have to be the smartest, nor does he/she have to come up with the best ideas. His/her most important job is to drive focus. The leader must cut through the noise and create a unifying, clear agenda.

2. Unless you understand the context, resolving issues can be a challenge. Categorizing issues under the right Cohegic facet can help you resolve issues in the appropriate manner.

3. Organizational issues are never-ending. A leader must create a larger context for the organization, so it looks beyond the small stuff.

Personal Takeaways

1. No one is perfect. Don't drink your own Kool-Aid. Intellectual brilliance is no guarantee against being dead wrong. Becoming self-aware is one of the most important traits of a good leader.

2. Manage your emotions, especially anger. Business and personal transformation are equally important.

3. We abuse our minds by making it work non-stop. Just like our body, our mind needs regular rest. Sleeping, watching TV, and exercising are insufficient. You must take time out at the end of the day to let your mind unwind. This simple act will change you.

Trent's Notes

Cohegic Method Takeaways

1. The five facets that cover all the elements of managing a business are:

   • Spirit, Direction, Engine, Execution, Cohesion

2. Understanding the five facets and their interaction as a system is a necessity for leading and managing an organization coherently.

3. The components of the five facets are:

   • Spirit: Mission, Core Management Philosophies, Values

   • Direction: Vision, Goals, Strategies

   • Engine: Work Processes, Organization Design, Culture

   • Execution: Measurement

4. An organization must cycle through the dynamic facets of direction, engine, and execution.

5. In each cycle, the organization must advance its strategy, and improve its engine and execution — transform continuously and systematically.

6. As it cycles, the organization must maintain cohesion among the dynamic facets and the static facet spirit.

Section 3: Spirit

Chapters in the Spirit section:

Cohegic Method

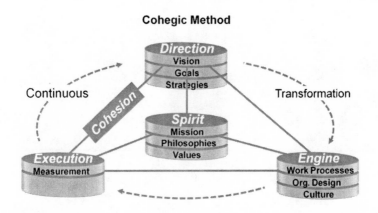

Chapter 6: Mission

Trent went to see the VP of HR. "Do you have a few minutes," asked Trent as he entered Oscar's office.

"Sure."

Trent closed the door and took a seat. He slowly tapped his fingers on the desk. Oscar waited for him to speak.

Finally, Trent said what he had come for, "Would you investigate Maxell's actions prior to the board meeting?"

"I was thinking of that myself," said Oscar, agreeing quickly to investigate the VP of marketing's actions. "We need to find out if Maxell spread those rumors and why."

Trent thanked Oscar and left.

"How're you doing?" asked Watson that evening, as he and Trent settled down on the patio chairs on the deck.

"I'm doing… okay. Yesterday's discussion weighed on me. I needed time to process it, but I feel better today."

As a mockingbird sang in the distance, Watson asked, "Do you want to discuss the personal issues or the method."

"Let's discuss the method."

"All right, let me share how we'll proceed. As we discuss each facet of the Cohegic method in detail, we'll apply it to Hintec and crystallize the related components."

"We'll crystallize Hintec's mission, strategy, and other artifacts?"

"Yes, and that'll be your first cycle."

"How much time will it take to implement the method?"

"It's an eternal process. I think your question is how much time the first cycle will take?"

"Yes."

"It's important to go through the first cycle as quickly as possible because this is change management and your probability of success diminishes the longer you take."

"Can we be done before the next board meeting in the second week of October… ten weeks from now?"

"Yes, if you and your team commit."

"I'm putting all my faith in your method. I hope I can present them with a coherent Hintec and a new me."

"I appreciate your faith, but one word of caution, neither the method nor I are perfect. But business isn't about perfection; it's about progress. As we get into the details, adopt what you like, and consider the rest with an open mind."

"You're hedging," said Trent raising his eyebrow.

"No. A good physician tells the patient what risks to expect. I don't want you to lose faith and give up mid-stream."

Trent shook his head. "I won't give up."

"All right then, let's jump right into it," said Watson, sitting up. "From what I can tell, Hintec does not have its spirit well-thought-out. Crystallizing spirit should be your first step."

"You had described spirit as…,"

"As the foundation, the soul. It defines the DNA, the passion, the reason for the organization's existence. The crisper the definition of spirit the stronger the organization, leaving no room for misinterpretation in the minds of the stakeholders."

"A weak soul isn't good for business," said Trent tongue-in-cheek.

Glad to see Trent in better spirits, Watson smiled and continued, "Spirit is meant to be static because if it changes it results in a different type of organization. Any change in spirit causes a cascade of dramatic changes in the other facets. If you find Hintec's spirit changing rapidly, it may indicate Hintec hasn't figured out what it wants to be — an identity crisis."

Trent deliberated on Watson's statement. "You've piqued my interest. I'm curious to crystallize Hintec's spirit."

"Crystallizing Hintec's spirit will be an eye-opener for you and your team," said Watson stoking Trent's curiosity.

"What do we have to crystallize?" asked Trent eagerly.

"The three components of mission, core management philosophies, and values,"

"I understand mission and values, what're philosophies?"

"We'll get into that, but first we must start with the mission because it sets the stage for the rest of the discussion on spirit."

"Okay," said Trent, paying attention.

"Mission describes the passion, the purpose behind the organization. What is Hintec's purpose?"

"Making money, of course," said Trent instantly.

Watson waved his index finger to disagree.

Trent looked at him doubtfully.

Watson explained, "Making money is one purpose, but it's not the main purpose behind why Hintec exists."

"Sure, it is," insisted Trent.

"No, it's not," Watson stood his ground. "There's a million ways to make money. Why is Hintec in your particular business?"

Trent thought about it.

Watson elaborated, "The founders of any company create it to serve a purpose close to their hearts and minds, which often relates to their experience and/or desire. The mission captures that inspiration and motivation."

While Trent cogitated, Watson continued, "The mission is an invitation to others to join and/or support the organization if they identify with the mission and are excited about it. It's the common thread tying all the employees."

"Hmm, I hadn't thought of it in those terms. I like that point very much. It's powerful to think about a company as a mission train. You decide if you want to jump on board. What's a good example of a mission statement?"

"Google says its mission is to organize the world's information and make it universally accessible and useful."

"That's succinct."

"Yes, it is. It reflects their desire to organize the immense amount of information available on the internet."

"Is Google's mission too specific?"

"When a statement's specific it has higher information content. Generic statements lack the power to move people. A specific mission could become limiting as a company grows, but Google's is fairly broad, and yet, defines Google quite well."

"You're right," said Trent, "mission statements often read we want to be the best company to invest in, the best supplier for our customers, the number one in customer service, and the best employer. It doesn't say much about the passion and purpose behind the company."

"You hit the nail on the head. Any other company could use the same words."

"Couldn't Google's mission statement be copied?"

"Sure, but those companies would need to become replicas of Google. To achieve the performance level we're talking about takes hard work in all the five facets. You can copy the mission but it's not easy to duplicate the passion."

"That's true. I have one doubt, though. It bothers me the founders are the ones who come up with the mission, and then it can't be changed."

"You don't have to cast the mission statement in stone. You may update it, but I hope you appreciate it's not something you change every Monday morning. At all times, the mission must reflect the purpose and passion driving the company."

"I think Hintec's mission has been lost in the day-to-day fire fighting," confessed Trent. "I'll go read our mission statement. The fact that I can't remember it, says a lot."

Watson nodded knowingly.

Trent concluded, "Hintec needs a specific mission statement that is a rally-cry for our employees."

"Do you have a second," asked Trent's assistant, the next morning.

"Sure, come in," said Trent.

Amy sat down and said, "How're you doing?"

"I'm doing well... why?"

"I was concerned for you yesterday. You seemed distant."

"Yeah, I know. I feel much better now. I'm getting back in the swing of things."

Trent went to see the VP of sales. After he sat down he said, "The board feels we've hit a plateau with new sales. How can we cross $30 million this quarter?"

Simon deliberated and then said, "The five new salespeople are on the ground running. They're raising the level of energy in the team. I'll push as hard as I can and re-double my effort to close bigger deals."

"We need more than hard work," said Trent, as he got up.

Simon nodded, but wasn't sure what Trent meant. He decided it was best not to ask.

In the evening, Trent returned to see his advisor. After they sat down, Trent pulled out a sheet and read Hintec's mission statement, "Hintec's mission is to serve our customers to the best of our abilities and create maximum value for them."

"How would you improve it?" tested Watson.

"This statement has the flaws we discussed. It's generic and you can't tell the passion or purpose behind Hintec."

"What is Hintec's passion?"

"…Helping customers make better decisions through our business-intelligence capabilities."

"If you were to design a new statement, what would it say?"

Trent thought for a minute. "To help our clients improve their strategy and operations through the use of our state-of-the-art business-intelligence software solutions."

"Is that what drives and energizes Hintec?"

"It is!" said Trent energetically.

"Good, then your new mission statement would accomplish its purpose. Now, let me ask you, is the mission statement true? Does Hintec live by this notion?"

"No," said Trent. Then he shared his read on the situation, "We mainly think about our software, and deal with customer issues so we can get the customers off our back. I'll admit we only think of customers when we want to sell more to them. We're not focused on improving their business."

"Then why did you say all of that in your new mission statement," pushed Watson.

"When you asked me to think of the mission, it was clear our passion is to help clients succeed. Unfortunately, because of the daily fire fighting, we've forgotten our real purpose."

Watson smiled, knowing Trent had taken his first step toward understanding what he needed to do different.

Running his hand through his thick hair, Trent continued, "This is amazing. Only when you asked me to stop, think, and write down the passion, did it become clear to me. I'm surprised it didn't occur to me or the others to stop and think about it."

"Happens all the time," said Watson.

"Passion, passion, passion. It's my new mantra."

"Passion and purpose are the company's North Star. Share the new statement with your team and incorporate their input. I recommend inviting a small random group of employees to participate and contribute to the discussion. Over time, you'll develop a powerful and inspiring statement."

When he returned home, Lori was in the bedroom with Catherine. Ethan had already gone to bed, and Debra was watching TV upstairs.

Trent picked up Catherine, cuddled her, and gave her a kiss. "I'm excited about our new mission statement," he told Lori, as he put Catherine down. "I hope it'll get everyone fired up."

"Great," she said. "Looks like you're making progress."

"Well, I've begun. I wonder how the team's going to respond to implementing the Cohegic method."

"You haven't asked them yet?"

"No, I'll do it next Monday, in the management meeting."

The VP of HR came to visit Trent the next morning. After taking a seat, Oscar said, "We've completed our investigation about Maxell."

"That's a fast turnaround. I asked you to investigate only a couple of days back."

"It's a sensitive issue which needed immediate attention."

"What are the findings?"

"Maxell spoke to several employees at the director and VP level and implied you would be relieved at the board meeting. He also disparaged your leadership style."

"What does Maxell have to say?" asked Trent, concerned.

"He admitted to these acts and realizes he acted unprofessionally, but still maintains you aren't the right leader."

"What's the next step?"

"Make a decision. Do you want to provide a warning, discipline him, or relieve him? You don't have to decide now."

Trent thought about it and said, "This issue is about culture. As VP of HR, you're the best guardian of culture.

Since I was involved in the incident, I recuse myself from this decision. You're the best person to make the decision."

"Okay. I recommend we relieve Maxell."

Trent paused, surprised at the quick decision by Oscar, and then said, "I agree with your recommendation. Would you let him know on Friday?"

"You look happy," said Lori, when Trent walked in.

"Yup, I'm happy. We decided to fire Maxell. I'm hungry, what do we have for dinner?"

"Cajun pasta." She narrowed her brow, "I thought you didn't have the power to fire Maxell. Didn't you say that the night before Catherine was born?"

"How can you remember things so minutely?"

Lori took the dinner plates out of the cabinet and Trent helped her set them on the table.

"When I was acting alone I didn't have the power to go against the board and the team to fire Maxell. Watson has taught me how to look at issues in the right perspective and employ the right resources. Having Oscar make the recommendation gave us combined the authority to make this decision."

After dinner, Trent walked over to Watson's house. It was later than usual and the sun had set. Martha was writing a letter in the office, so they sat in the living room.

"Oscar decided to let Maxell go," said Trent, beaming.

"Did you ask him why he made that decision?"

"No, I didn't."

"I can appreciate that. You're feeling vindicated, but Maxell's lost his livelihood. It's worth thinking about what he's going through. Your team's going to watch your body language carefully to see if this was about retaliation. The manner in which you present this news is important."

Early next morning, Trent went to see Oscar.

"We shouldn't wait to share the news about Maxell until the management meeting on Monday. Instead, after you tell Maxell, would you visit with each VP and explain the rationale behind the decision."

"Okay," said Oscar.

"Because we're relieving Maxell for cause we're not contractually obligated to pay severance. However, I want us to pay him a severance and provide outplacement help."

Oscar beamed. "Excellent suggestions."

Trent waited a minute, and then asked, "What was the reason behind your decision?"

"Maxell crossed the line. He attempted to create a referendum on you; buoyed by the hope his effort would become a grass-root initiative. But, in order to do so, he lied. He misrepresented how board members felt about you. Hintec must foster difference of opinion, but we can't condone lies, manipulation, and malicious behavior. We had to send a clear message; unprofessional behavior won't be tolerated."

Just before closing time, Oscar stopped to see Trent. "The VPs understand the decision, and appreciate your gesture of providing severance. Even Hector agreed it was the right decision."

"How did Maxell receive the news?"

"He was expecting it. I explained the severance package and the help we'd provide him. After our meeting, he quietly packed his belongings and left without talking to anyone."

"Thank you for taking care of this, Oscar."

"Sure, have a great weekend."

"Honey, I'm home," said Trent as he walked in.

"How was your day?" asked Lori turning toward him.

"We let Maxell go."

"Did he take it okay?"

"Maxell had admitted lying and so was expecting it."

"Maxell lied about what?"

"That the board was going to fire me."

"Didn't you lie about firing Maxell?"

Trent searched his mind for an answer. Lori realized she probably shouldn't have asked that question.

"Yes, I did. Should I be fired too?" he asked, mulling.

"I wasn't going there," said Lori. "Let's change the subject."

"No, it's all right," he said, willing to face the difficult question. "Maxell made a huge mistake in stirring up trouble that violated the office environment. I made a serious mistake too, albeit not of the same magnitude. I paid for my deeds by going through the humiliation and loss of authority at the board meeting," he said somberly.

Lori changed the subject.

The next morning, Trent went to see Watson. It being a sunny morning, they sat outside on the deck. The choppy waves thrashed against the wooden embankment around the lake.

"Watson, I've seen you almost every day for two weeks. To top it, I'm here again on a Saturday."

"As long as you don't ask me to be involved on a full-time basis, I'm happy to do this. Tell me what's happening."

"We let Maxell go. Oscar explained the decision to the team and he reported they were okay with the decision."

Watson nodded his approval. "Using Oscar was the right thing and the smart thing to do. How did Oscar explain the reason to fire Maxell?"

"Maxell had lied and his conduct was unacceptable."

"While I'm sorry for Maxell, I'm happy for Hintec. Oscar's a mature individual. Through him, Hintec has demonstrated it upholds its values seriously."

"I guess we need to define Hintec's values."

"We will," said Watson.

"See if Hector's available," Trent asked Amy on Monday morning. "I'd like to see him before the management meeting."

A few minutes later, the VP of customer service walked in. As he sat own, Trent said, "I hope you understand the reason why we let Maxell go, and don't see it as a vindictive move on my part."

"Oscar explained everything to me," said Hector. "I apologize for my outburst. I didn't know what Maxell had done. He didn't include me in his little campaign; otherwise, I would've stopped him. I'm sorry I jumped to conclusions."

Happy to hear Hector's apology, Trent said, "I wasn't much of a hero myself. I've learned my lesson, and I hope I'm able to improve my relationship with you."

"I'd like that. I look forward to working with you in a more collegial manner," said Hector.

The puckered faced and brusque Hector suddenly didn't seem as menacing as before, making Trent a little more comfortable. "I need your help to improve our client retention rate," said Trent, perhaps asking for the first time, instead of demanding.

Hector paused. Then he said, "I'll talk to my team and ask them to ensure they don't let things fall through the cracks like it happened in the case of Zucor Energy. I'll also review the knowledge-level of our customer service reps."

Trent was pleased to have Hector's cooperation.

At the management meeting, after they had attended to the regular agenda items, Trent said, "I mentioned last week about my advisor, Watson. He's helping me understand his Cohegic method, so we can implement it here."

"Have we made a decision to implement it?" asked Fran.

Trent hesitated. "Yes, I made that decision…."

"Why," interjected Hector. "What will it do for us?"

"It'll give us a systematic manner to connect all our decisions and initiatives. Help us think coherently."

"How do you know it'll work?" pressed Hector. "How's Watson qualified?"

"I can't guarantee it'll work, but as you'll see, it's intuitive and conceptual. I've developed a lot of faith in Watson. I'm confident his method will help us. Even in my first discussion with him on mission, I've seen the value of his counsel."

Trent looked at Hector and Fran. They didn't look convinced. He looked at Oscar, Venkat, and Simon, who looked noncommittal. Trent felt his blood boil and his heart racing. He clenched his fist and said with a raised voice, "Guys!"

Everyone looked at him with tense expressions. Trent saw the tense faces and took a deep breath to calm himself. "We've got to do something different. Give me a chance. Do I know if Watson's method will work? I don't, but I've become comfortable with him. He's making sense." He stopped and looked around. No one spoke. "Please," he urged, "I need your support." Then he looked at Oscar, "Can you support me?"

"Yes, we can," answered Oscar, in a firm voice.

Fran and Hector looked at Oscar.

"Trent is right," said Oscar, "we should try something different. If it doesn't work, we'll be wiser for having tried it."

"What is the Cohegic method?" asked Venkat.

Trent displayed the Cohegic diagram on the screen and explained the five facets, and the need to transform continuously by cycling through them.

"What you've described is at a high level," said Hector, unsure about the value of the method.

"As we discuss the facets in detail and develop their components, we'll get to where the rubber meets the road."

"We should pursue it," reiterated Oscar, more to support Trent than as an endorsement of what he had heard.

Fran, Simon, and Venkat nodded their tentative support.

"Thank you," said Trent, seizing the approvals. "I'm eager to make rapid progress," he pushed. "My sense is we'll need to devote considerable time. Let's meet for an hour every day or every other day, till we're done with the first cycle."

"Let's have an off-site retreat to get it done," suggested Fran.

"It's best if we have time between the meetings. It'll allow us to percolate on our discussions. I'm eager to make it happen soon, but I don't want to rush it unduly. Watson has reminded me, patience and thoroughness are virtues."

Oscar smiled.

Trent continued, "I'll ask Amy to schedule a series of meetings, and schedule the first one for 4:00 PM today, if it fits with your schedules. Also, we'll invite a different group of ten employees to each meeting so they can contribute."

"That's a great idea," said Oscar.

After the meeting, Trent called Amy into his office.

"We're going to implement a coherent method to manage Hintec," said Trent. "It'll require the management team to devote considerable time over the next few weeks. Coordinate with the other admins to make room on their calendars."

"We can get time on their calendars. It's your calendar I'm concerned about," said Amy.

"This is my highest priority," he stressed. "To each meeting invite a different group of ten randomly selected employees. Here's a handout to distribute to the employees prior to the meetings. It has an overview of the method, a letter from me and some information about my advisor."

"Thanks for coming," Trent said that afternoon looking at the employees. "As you may have read in the handout, we're kicking off the implementation of a coherent method to manage Hintec." He looked briefly at Fran and Oscar. "Today we need to develop our mission statement. What is our passion?"

Several around the table spoke at once. To produce the best business-intelligence software; to ensure our clients are satisfied; to be the fastest growing software firm.

"Let me rephrase. Why do we exist?" clarified Trent.

Other voices joined in. To make money; to make the world a better place; to serve our customers; to serve our employees.

"I appreciate the answers," said Trent, "but, they aren't clicking. Think about what is our mission. What's our purpose?"

"To help our customers," said one employee.

"You're right," said Trent energized. "The question is what help our customers are looking for, and how do we help them?

After a minute of pause, another employee said, "Our clients have all the data, but they have no intelligence. They can't piece the data together and make sense of it. Our mission is to help them make intelligent decisions."

Around the table, eyes lit up, and several murmured, "Yeah."

"It has a good ring. Our mission's to help clients make better decisions," said Trent. "The more specific a statement, the more powerful it is. Tell me what decisions we help clients make?"

"We can help them with any decision," said a software engineer. "What are their costs and expenses? Where do their revenues come from? Which products are performing well? Which market segments are doing well?"

"Good, but these are information points," said Trent.

"Their decision questions are: Where to employ capital? Which markets and products deserve focus? Which areas require improvement in cost efficiency?" offered Fran.

Several nodded.

Trent got up and walked to the white board. He wrote down, "Our mission is to leverage our capabilities, experience, and technology, to help our clients make faster and better quality, strategic and operational decisions based on accurate and complete business-intelligence."

He looked around the table. "Let me ask the management team what they think. They have been quiet."

"Very good," said Oscar.

"I think it's powerful," said Hector.

"What is our current mission statement," asked Fran.

"We will serve our customers to the best of our abilities and create maximum value for them," replied Trent.

"That doesn't say much," said Fran.

"You're right," said Trent, "unlike the old mission, the new one says exactly what we do, why we exist. Further, the statement isn't overly specific; it doesn't tie us down. Do you think our new statement adequately captures our passion?"

"Yes, our passion is to see our clients succeed," said Oscar.

Several others agreed.

"Okay," Trent said, "I'll ask the marketing team to take a look at it and refine it if necessary. Do we have a mission which will motivate us and our co-workers?"

"That may be asking for a lot," said Hector. "I like the new statement, but I wouldn't expect miracles."

Oscar stepped in, "I agree, it'll take some time for employees to fully appreciate it and connect with it."

After dinner, Trent went to show Watson the new mission statement. When he rang the doorbell, Martha opened the door. Watson was in his office reading a business magazine. Trent joined him, and they sat at the round table.

As he sat down, Trent said, "I reminded Hector this morning to focus on client retention, our most immediate and pressing problem. Can you help me with it?"

"Yes, of course, I'll help you. But I want to help you through the means of the method; otherwise, you'll go back to addressing issues in an ad-hoc, piecemeal manner. Concentrate on the method and we'll systematically answer all your issues including client retention, and ensure all the answers fit cohegically."

"Okay. We developed our new mission statement." He handed Watson a sheet of paper.

Watson read it. "Looks good. What did your team think?"

"They liked it, but it didn't generate any immediate vows of commitment. I had hoped this would get them motivated."

The mission statement will come alive when you breathe life into it. You'll have to repeat the mission a thousand times for it to become second nature to your people, and for them to start identifying with the mission."

"I'll be the chief cheerleader for the mission," said Trent, enjoying the moment.

"Very good. Now remember, this is only the first step. The challenge is to extrapolate the mission through every aspect of Hintec. Toward that goal, we have to crystallize an extremely important component of spirit — Hintec's core management philosophies. The choices you make there will determine Hintec's destiny."

Trent's Notes

Cohegic Method Takeaways

1. It is nearly impossible to drive clarity unless you crystallize the spirit of the organization. The spirit facet (mission, philosophies and values) is the soul, the DNA, the foundation of the organization.

2. In many companies, the mission statement provides little value and the organization overlooks it. To create a strong sense of commitment, the mission statement must capture the passion and purpose of the organization, so it becomes an invitation for people to join the bandwagon.

3. Often, the mission statement is a general and generic statement that could easily apply to other companies. Your mission statement must be as specific as possible, so when people read it they can immediately associate it with your company.

Trent's Notes

Management and Leadership Takeaways

1. In engineering, perfection is most important. In business, progress is far more important than perfection.

2. A leader must repeat the mission statement a thousand times for it to become second nature to the organization — constantly reminding all the stakeholders about the purpose of the organization.

3. A business leader gains more power when he/she leverages the appropriate resources, and is sensitive when dealing with organizational issues.

Hintec's Old Mission Statement

Hintec's mission is to serve our customers to the best of our abilities and create maximum value for them.

Hintec's New Mission Statement

Our mission is to leverage our business-intelligence capabilities, knowledge, and state-of-the-art technology, to help our clients make faster and better quality, strategic and operational decisions based on accurate and complete business-intelligence.

Chapter 7: Core Management Philosophies

When Trent reached his advisor's home, the door was ajar. He knocked lightly. Watson opened the door. "Come in. Our grandkids are here, but they're leaving. Why don't you head to the deck and I'll join you."

Trent headed out. Watson joined him soon thereafter. After Watson sat down, Trent shared, "I showed the mission statement to my assistant. While she didn't think it was a rah-rah statement, she felt it articulated well our purpose."

"Good. You've set the overall context through your mission statement. Now you must further define the context so it leaves no room for misinterpretation."

"I'm ready to go."

"By defining the core management philosophies you'll define the guiding principles. The choice of core philosophies will deeply impact Hintec from its culture to its competencies."

"Are core philosophies the strategy?"

"Philosophies are at a higher level. You may change your strategies, but your core philosophies will remain the same regardless of internal or external conditions."

"Do you have an example?"

"Wal-Mart's core philosophies are operational efficiency, lower prices, and high volume. Wal-Mart may change its strategies to get into product areas such as groceries, liquor, gas stations, and health-care, or get out of them. But whichever product-line they choose, their approach to leveraging their technology and supply-chain expertise will remain constant."

"I see what you're saying."

"Mediocre companies do a poor job of crystallizing and sticking to their core philosophies. Successful companies carefully craft core philosophies and stick to them."

"Do you have more examples of core philosophies?"

"Sure. Product experience is BMW's core philosophy. BMW has built a brand and a company around providing its customer the best driving experience. Amazon's philosophy is to be an on-line retailer. That's where its capabilities and processes shine. Opening brick-and-mortar retail centers will go against its grain. For McDonalds and Subway, convenience, consistency, and low prices are the core philosophies. You won't find an expensive, fine-dining McDonalds."

"That's true. What should be Hintec's philosophies?"

"We'll identify them, but there's a category of philosophies you need to understand first, the business model. To make decision-making clearer, Hintec must methodically select and adopt one of these three business models: product-centric, client-centric, or operations-centric."

"You would have to select all three models," argued Trent, recognizing that all three are important and necessary.

"To an extent, yes. Hintec can't afford to do poorly in any of the three areas. However, it must pick one in which it will be absolutely great, and make sure it is good enough in the other two. It'd be difficult to be great in all three because that'd mean you wouldn't be focused on any one."

"So it's a question about selecting Hintec's emphasis and overall focus," clarified Trent.

"Yes. Clearly picking one model is important because the models conflict in many aspects," explained Watson. "For instance, operationally focused companies typically charge lower prices, while product leaders charge a premium."

"What are the three models again?"

"Product, client and operations-centric. Let's understand them one by one. Operations-centric companies focus on efficiency and quality. They provide products and services at the most competitive prices, in the most reliable manner. They're leaders in cost control and time management."

"Wal-Mart and Southwest Airlines?"

"Yes, they're great examples of operations-centric companies. Intel, Sony and Apple on the other hand are product-centric. These types of companies bring the most innovative, differentiating products to the marketplace. Customers often pay a premium to purchase their products."

"BMW, Boeing, and Lexus?"

"Them too. And, last, client-centric companies invest huge amounts of time and energy to understand each individual client. Knowledge of their client's specific issues allows them to provide solutions tailored to the client's needs. Brokerage firms, custom home builders, lawyers and physicians are good examples."

"I get it. These models represent three completely different types of companies. So, what should be Hintec's model?"

"A company-defining question for your management team, board and you to answer."

In the next meeting, after Trent explained the three business models, he asked, "So which model best applies to us?"

"Product-centric obviously," said Simon, the VP of sales.

"I agree," said Venkat. Hector and Fran nodded as well.

"I agree with you all. We want to create the best product and stay at the forefront of technology. That is why the engineering department is so important to us," said Trent, looking at Venkat.

"Thank you," said Venkat. "By the way, I shared the new mission statement with my team, and they really liked it."

"Mine too," said Oscar. "They didn't get excited enough to jump on their chairs, but they liked it."

"Very funny," said Trent.

Everyone laughed.

Simon came to see Trent. "I have unconfirmed reports that GenceSoft may be starting a price war," he shared.

"A price war? Are you sure?"

"I'm not sure. It could just be a handful of deals to make their numbers for the quarter."

Trent looked down at the table thinking, and then said, "They're big enough to suffocate us out of business... but we may be too small for them to worry about."

"I'll investigate further and let you know," offered Simon. "It might take me at least a couple of weeks. It's hard to get the inside scoop on their deals."

"Let me know as soon as you find out more."

"The team picked product leadership," shared Trent with Watson, when he saw him in the evening.

"Did your team consider client-centric?"

"No, we're out-and-out a product company," said Trent firmly.

"Your mission states your purpose is to help customers make better decisions. Isn't your product just the means?"

"What do you mean?" said Trent raising his eyebrows.

"Can you... I'm being harsh here, throw your software over the fence, hoping the customers figure out how best to use it?"

"Oh, but we train the customers."

"You train them on?"

"On using the software."

"You train customers on your product, but not on solving their problems. Isn't there a lot more the customers must do to solve their problems?"

"Yes, they must ensure the raw data's accurate; make sure they're collecting the right type of data; make sure management reads and uses the analysis. There's a lot that must happen."

Trent paused in thought. Watson waited.

"You're right, our approach has been from the product's perspective, not the customer's. And, by customer I don't mean the user of our software, but the entire client organization."

"For Hintec, client-centric makes the most sense because you must care about each individual client and ensure they succeed. Similar to a law firm, or a CPA firm."

Trent shook his head. "We're not a consulting firm. If we hold our customer's hands, we won't be able to serve many customers. We want to grow rapidly." He stopped and looked at the lake. "I need to sleep on this. Tomorrow, I've a lunch appointment with the Chief Information Officer of one our clients. I'll ask him for feedback."

"Wonderful idea. It's always good to ask clients."

Trent and Simon had a meeting the next morning. After the meeting, as Simon began to leave, Trent said, "Oh, Simon."

Simon stopped and looked back at Trent.

"Would you see us as client-centric?"

"Nope," said Simon without batting an eyelid, "we're a product company, and will always be one."

"You're right. There may be some merit to us being client centric, but overwhelmingly we're a product company. I have a lunch appointment with Kyle Jared today. I'll ask him."

"Please don't," said Simon. "We don't want to confuse our clients. Moreover Kyle's a CIO, he'll pick product-centric."

Trent took Kyle to his favorite seafood restaurant. Both men ordered sea bass. While they waited for the food to arrive, Trent said, "I need your perspective on a matter."

"Sure, go ahead."

"Should Hintec be client or product-centric?"

"It's interesting you should ask that. I'm under pressure. In our industry, technology is a critical competitive differentiator. My CEO sees IT as a business partner instead of just providing low-level computer services."

"Are you involved in strategy and operations?"

"Absolutely," said Kyle. "And, I need software vendors who understand our business and can provide solutions that are specifically tailored to our needs."

Trent took that as a vote for being client-centric.

That afternoon as Trent was working his phone rang. It was the Chairman. "Hello Trent, this is Cedric."

"Good afternoon, sir. How're you doing?"

"I'm fine, thanks. I called about the mission statement."

"What do you think?" asked Trent, slightly nervous.

"I like it. It's simple and states our purpose well."

"Thanks for the feedback."

"How're things going?" probed Cedric.

"I'm working closely with Watson. He's challenging me to question my assumptions. Speaking about which, do you think we should be product-centric or client-centric?"

"We should be both."

"I agree. But if we needed to be great in one and good enough in the other, which would you pick?"

"Do we need to pick one as more important?"

"Watson tells me picking one will allow us to focus better and get more bang-for-the-buck for our efforts and resources."

Cedric was silent for a minute. "When I started Hintec I knew nothing about technology. I still don't. I focused on how we could help customers make better decisions."

"Of course… and that's what we put in our new mission statement as well," said Trent.

"But over time as the product became more complex, we focused more on the product and less on the customer. Barry being a technologist understood the product more than he understood the customer."

"So going forward, which one would you recommend?"

"Client-centric first, and then product-centric."

"I appreciate your advice," said Trent. "Thank you,"

That evening Trent began. "I talked to my client, and Cedric. Both leaned toward client-centric… but I'm not

100% sure. This isn't an easy choice," said Trent shaking his head.

"If you want to stay product-centric, make your product as simple to operate as a car, like a car manufacturer does, or as simple to use as tax preparation software, like Intuit does."

"I will admit our product is complex. Complexity could be one of the reasons behind our high customer turn-over."

Trent got up and walked over to the railing. Watson joined him. Looking beyond his lawn, out over the lake, Watson said, "Your product isn't a pill clients can consume and feel better. In its current manifestation, your product is an invasive surgery. It requires special and intimate care of the client."

"Even if we made our product simple to use, we'd still have the challenge of changing the client organization's processes. We can't assume clients will be able to benefit from it fully."

"That's my point."

"What concerns me is, won't a high-touch, client-centric model produce slower growth than a low-touch model?"

"If you do it well, you'll grow. Look at homebuilders. Building low to mid-end, cookie-cutter, tract homes can offer much higher growth rates in number of homes built, compared to building high-end, custom homes."

"I see the point," said Trent. "The custom home builder could still generate much more profits at a lower volume."

"Indeed," said Watson, "the total profit depends on how well the homebuilders execute either business model. You're looking for 20% growth with a lower client turnover rate. A client-centric model could help you achieve that in a healthy fashion."

Night was falling and a breeze came over the water. The men returned to their chairs under the protection of the balcony.

"Can you appreciate why the organization gets confused when philosophies aren't clearly identified?" said Watson.

"I see that," said Trent, nodding vigorously. "I have a question. If we become client-centric then shouldn't we be willing to use any product to meet the customer's needs."

"I like your question. The idea's not to abandon your product, but to stand on top of it and create a lot more value. Being client-centric will help you make your product superior."

"You mean in terms of our ability to help our clients make better decisions."

"Exactly, and my bet is you'll end up not with the best product, but with the best solution for your clients."

"As I think about the other companies in our space, they strike me as product-centric," mused Trent. "Being client-centric could become our competitive advantage. One more question. You said companies must keep their philosophies static, but wouldn't Hintec be changing its philosophy, and what stops the next CEO from changing it again?"

"Great question. Becoming client-centric will require significant effort, and once you adopt it you won't be able to change it easily. That's the rub. Philosophies aren't holy. You can change them, but doing so is excruciating. So you, and the CEO's after you, better have a good reason to change them."

When he got home, the house was quiet and the lights dim. He walked softly towards the master bedroom. Lori was nursing Catherine. She gestured him to be quiet. Catherine finished nursing, and Lori put her in the crib. As Catherine had fallen asleep, they went out to sit on the back porch.

"Mom's getting ready to go home," said Lori.

"Did you ask her to stay longer?"

"I did, but didn't convince her. How was your meeting?"

"Insightful. Our philosophies until now had developed by default, without any deliberate thinking. I'm learning how important it is to clearly think through and define them."

Trent was in his office the next day when the phone rang. He answered.

"Cedric's in the office. He wants to see you," said Amy.

Trent walked down the hall to the boardroom. Cedric used it as an office when he was on site. Once Trent took a seat, Cedric said, "I recently met Clay Armstrong, the CEO of ExeSoft, a HR software company, based in west Houston. Clay started ExeSoft seven years ago and has grown it rapidly."

"How big is the company now?"

"Six hundred million in revenues."

"That's impressive growth."

"I was thinking about inviting Clay to join our board. Would you look into him and ExeSoft? Having him on our board might be helpful to you. I want to know your thoughts."

"I'll check him out and let you know," said Trent.

"Today's discussion on philosophies probably requires just the management team's deliberations. I didn't invite anyone else," started Trent in his meeting.

"Last time we agreed product-centric is our business model, but my discussion with Watson, Cedric and three of our clients has made me realize our model should be client-centric."

Venkat voiced his objection, "That doesn't make sense."

"Doesn't make sense to me either," quickly followed Simon, "I thought we had already discussed this."

"I don't want to force my thoughts on you. I'll do my best to make a case to show you why it makes sense."

"We appreciate your tenor," said the VP of HR. Turning to Venkat and Simon, Oscar added, "I'm sure we'll keep an open mind."

"Until now," Trent continued, "we've pushed our product without finding out how much our clients benefit. Are we…."

Simon interrupted, "Our customers benefit a lot, otherwise they wouldn't be renewing."

Trent winced. "80% renewal is nothing to be proud of." He looked around the table. "Do our customers truly benefit? Do they truly improve their decision-making?"

"We aren't baby-sitters!" asserted Simon. "We shouldn't bog ourselves down in our customer's business. We can't even handle the existing service calls, how do we expect to do more?"

Trent frowned but let the VP of sales continue.

"Our customers spend millions on our software," said Simon. "They know what they're doing. Let's follow the lite approach: develop the product, train the users, and let the customers do their thing."

The CFO countered, "Our customers aren't experts in business-intelligence; we are. Our product and this field is complex. It's our responsibility to ensure they get value."

"I concur with Fran," said Venkat, reversing his stance. "Customers use our software marginally and even incorrectly. It amuses my team to see the data users load into our databases. The data is technically correct, but we can't see how you could generate any meaningful business insight from it. It's not a software training issue; it's about them understanding their own business, and understanding business-intelligence."

"You're right," said Fran.

"Also," added Trent, "they have issues in their organization; process and technology issues, politics...."

Venkat interjected, "This takes me back to the point I've made several times before. We've added features to create the wow factor, and not practical features that make our product usable and useful. There's been a problem in our thinking."

"Now, wait a minute," said Simon.

Trent waved a hand to stop him. "Let me expand on Venkat's point. The IT folks might understand our product, but the business executives don't comprehend its power. As I say this, it makes me realize how long we've overlooked this fundamental aspect. I've preached customer service, but my view of it was so narrow."

Trent stopped to look at Hector, but the VP of customer service didn't offer anything. Trent continued, "I suspect many of our problems stem from us being product-centric. Our high client turnover rate, our high volume of customer-issues, and our difficulty with our sales pitch all signal we're following the wrong philosophy."

"What's wrong with being product-centric?" pressed Simon.

"Let me clarify," replied Trent. "There's nothing wrong with product-centric. For many companies it makes sense, but at Hintec, we must help each individual client use our product, and ensure they gain substantial value from it."

Simon shook his head, disagreeing. "If we're that screwed up, how come 80% of our customers renew."

"Corporate inertia," replied Trent. "Companies often keep paying for things without analyzing how much it helps them."

Trent looked at Simon. Simon returned his gaze but didn't respond. Trent let out an exasperated breath. "Why do you think we lost Wesley Chemicals? They didn't see value in our product! And, Zucor... you remember we had that long discussion to find out what had gone wrong." Trent glanced at Hector and then looked back at Simon. "It was the same issue. Zucor didn't understand our product and how to use it."

"You have a point," replied Simon slowly, "once the sale is done, we act only as bystanders. We can recalibrate, but it's a big change, and it makes me nervous."

"Me too," said Trent. "Also, I'm assuming customers want our help. I've only asked three so far. We need to find out how they'll respond to our new approach." Turning to Hector, Trent said, "What do you think? You haven't said much."

Hector replied, "You're proposing a fundamental change. We don't have the skills to make that happen, not within our employee or management ranks. We'll have to hire people who can go into client organizations and help them."

Trent looked at the others and said, "Hector's right, the change is significant. It'll redefine our company, but it's the right change. We can and should make it happen."

"I like client-centric," said Oscar.

"I like it too," said Venkat. Fran nodded.

"This discussion's been very good," said Oscar. "Thank you, Trent, for making us think. Hintec will make great progress if we make this transition."

"Thanks, Oscar. Thank you all," said Trent letting out a deep breath.

Driving back home from work, Trent played the whole discussion with Watson and the team in his mind. He felt both excited about the potential of the new philosophy and apprehensive at the same time. After dinner, he went over to Watson's house.

Martha opened the door. "Hi, come in. Watson will be back soon. He went over to see the grandkids."

Trent walked out to the deck and sat down. He watched the waves. They were choppy and he watched the ducks flap their wings as they skimmed along the surface of the water.

Watson opened the glass door and came out. "Sorry to keep you waiting."

Startled, Trent looked up. "I was enjoying the lake."

"So, what's the news?" Watson asked as he sat down.

"The team after a long and good discussion adopted client-centric as our business model."

"That's great," said Watson, with a firm nod. "Client-centric is your first core philosophy. Now, can you think about other philosophies, other non-negotiable aspects of your business approach?"

Trent searched his mind.

"Why don't I ask you some questions and see if we uncover any other core choices?"

"Okay."

"How big is your market universe... the total dollars spent by all companies on business-intelligence products and services?"

"There are various estimates from $15 to $50 billion globally. At $200 million, we only have a small share, 2 to 3%."

"How fast is this market growing annually?"

"5 to 7%," answered Trent.

"Profile Hintec's preferred clients for me."

"Companies or business units of corporations with $100 million to $10 billion in revenues."

"Would your preference change if the competition focused on that segment or if it was succeeding in another segment?"

"No," replied Trent.

"If your preference won't change, maybe it's a core philosophy. Can you elaborate on your answer?"

"We want accounts that generate at least $1 million in annual revenues. It's easier to generate that from prospects in the $100 million to $10 billion revenue range."

Watson closed his eyes briefly as Trent continued.

"Today, we have hundreds of accounts smaller than $1 million, and that contributes to our chaos and poor service."

Rubbing his chin, Watson asked, "Would an economic downturn force you to abandon your preference? If your philosophy is subject to change, then it's more of a strategy."

"That's a good question. I need to give it more thought," said Trent. "Basically you're talking about market segmentation."

"It goes deeper. Companies use market segmentation to determine their product, sales and marketing thrust. It is part of their strategy, and shifts as they gauge the market response. What I'm talking about is defining the entire company around a specific market segment."

"Okay, I understand."

"Good," said Watson, standing up. "Martha and I are going to San Antonio with our daughter and grandkids for a quick summer get-away. We'll be back on Sunday."

"Okay, please have a wonderful trip."

When he reached home, Lori was watching TV in the family room. "What did you learn today?" she asked.

Trent smiled. "You're enjoying this, aren't you? You think I don't know much."

"Now, honey, you know I think highly of you. It's just that it's the job of a good spouse to keep pushing."

He wrinkled his nose at her, and came and sat next to her. She gave him a kiss.

Sitting back, he said, "Everything Watson asks is common sense. They're basic questions a company must ask itself. Sometimes, I wonder, why didn't the management team, the board, or I raise these questions? I guess we were so consumed by whatever we were doing, we didn't have the time... and maybe the interest in slowing down to ask them."

Trent went to see the VP of sales on Monday. Simon was working at his computer with his back towards the door. When he turned around, Trent asked, "Morning Simon. How's everything? Any info on GenceSoft?"

"No new info on their pricing tactics, but I did find out, NAPIT Oil has invited them to bid on the RFP."

"Drat," said Trent. "I thought NAPIT was only considering us. After all we helped them develop their need."

"I tried to find out what had changed, but NAPIT isn't talking, at least not for now. I'll keep working on them."

"Okay," said Trent thoughtfully. "I have a question." He stood, loosely holding the top of a chair's back. "Should we focus on $1 million accounts as a stated philosophy?"

"I'd think carefully before making it a hard and fast rule," said Simon, not liking the idea. "Some accounts start small and grow large."

"How many times has that happened?" pushed Trent.

"Many times!" said Simon waving his hand.

"What's the percentage?" pressed Trent.

Simon shrugged his shoulders. "Larger deals have longer sales cycle-times and lower success ratios. A $100,000 deal is easier to close than a $1 million deal. Do you really care where the dollars come from? You hold me accountable for total sales, not the size of each deal."

"Hmm… I need to think about this more."

"Okay," said Simon, with a concerned look on his face.

Trent turned around and walked out.

Next, Trent went to see the CFO.

"Do you have a minute?" he asked.

"I'm in the middle of something," said Fran.

"Come see me when you have a few minutes," said Trent.

Fran knocked on Trent's door later in the afternoon.

"Come in," said Trent. After she took a seat, he asked, "Should we focus only on $1 million annual revenue accounts?"

"We must see where 80% of our revenues come from. Let's go to my office, so I can check my computer."

They walked to her office. Fran sat down and printed two copies of a report. Giving a copy to Trent, she said, "As you can see, we have 578 accounts and $201.64 million in revenues. The top 25% of our accounts produce 61% of our revenues; the top 48% of accounts produce 82% of our revenues."

Trent spent time reviewing the revenue table.

"This is a great table. How come I haven't seen it before?"

Fran looked lost for a second. "You haven't asked for it."

After studying the report, Trent observed, "52% of our accounts are less than $250,000 each, and they contribute less than 20% of the total revenues."

"Does it take the same amount of sales effort to win a large account as a small account?" asked Fran.

"The effort required isn't that different. The consensus, however, is that it's easier to close a smaller account because it's easier to get the prospect to make a decision. But it may not just be the question of what we can sell... but what we can deliver."

"Good evening," said Watson as he opened the door that evening. "It's breezy outside, where would you like to sit?"

"I don't mind a breeze if it isn't too stiff."

"Okay, let's go out."

"How was San Antonio?" asked Trent.

"Wonderful. We had a lot of fun."

As they sat down, Trent said, "The idea of $1 million accounts is appealing but is it a philosophy. How do I tell if it should be a philosophy or a strategy?"

"A great question. Think about the example we discussed earlier about the custom home builders. What if a custom home builder that builds homes in the $3 million plus range starts building homes in the $300,000 range?"

"They could generate a lot of media buzz."

"Sure, but think about what the organization would have to go through to retool itself. Building homes in the $300,000 range is quite different from building homes in the $3 Million plus range."

As Trent deliberated, Watson said, "Let's take another example, Lexus and Toyota."

"Great example," jumped in Trent. "Doesn't Toyota offer several different models in different price ranges? Also, Toyota and Lexus are the same company."

Watson smiled. "Even though Toyota offers different models, they're all in the same genre. While the Toyota and Lexus brands are part of the same company, they target distinct market segments. A Lexus dealership will never sell a Toyota on its dealership lot, and an economic downturn won't force Lexus to change its luxury-market-segment philosophy."

"That's true."

"Combining the two brands would create confusion," continued Watson. "The expectations of customers of an entry level Toyota Corolla and a high-end Lexus LS 400 series are quite different. Distinct brands create clarity for the customers and for the organization. It becomes clear what the brand promises and what needs it fulfills."

"I understand the Toyota example, but in our case, the difference in how we serve the large and small accounts isn't that big. Should the account-size decision be part of an evolving strategy as opposed to a philosophy?"

"The answer lies in what you just said. Why isn't there much difference between how you serve the large and small accounts? Isn't it possible the larger accounts involve greater complexity and require a different level of understanding and effort? Are you short-changing the larger accounts by serving them at a level that's equivalent to the lowest common denominator?"

Trent sighed. "I suspect that's one of our problems. All we're providing upper-tier accounts is faster issue resolution."

"When you design the entire company around acquiring, serving, and growing upper-tier accounts, that's when it'll become an inherent philosophy and not a strategy."

"I get it, don't mix tiers," surmised Trent. "Should we develop two distinct brands?"

"Focus on only one for now."

Trent stopped and reflected. "Client-centric and upper-tier accounts, is a powerful combination for us. It could improve our customer retention and provide an impetus for growth. I can now see how the crystallization of philosophies does determine your company's destiny."

"Remember, identifying philosophies is only the beginning. Having the discipline to stick with them is the critical success factor. This is one area that'll seriously challenge and test your resolve."

"I feel pretty good about my discussions with Watson," said Trent as he lay on his bed staring at the ceiling.

Half asleep, Lori murmured, "That's good, honey."

"But I'm worried how we'll make the transition. Will we be able to reinvent ourselves? ...I need to prepare really well for the next board meeting." He continued staring at the ceiling. When he turned to look at her, she was asleep.

He got up and sat in the recliner to do the exercise Watson had recommended. Few minutes later, he returned to bed.

Trent started the next meeting, "I didn't invite a group of employees today as well, because I felt these philosophy discussions are a little sensitive. Do you have any feedback on our last meeting about core philosophies?"

"I spoke to one of my HR colleagues in the oil-field services business," said Oscar. "They're client-centric because every client of theirs has a different way of doing things, from the way they request bids, to how they award contracts and how they want the work executed. We're in a similar situation. Every client of ours has unique challenges and internal issues too."

"Exactly," said Trent. "And, we'll standardize as best as we can. But we have to recognize the special needs of each of our clients. Client-centric is right for us, and I hope it'll solve our retention problem. More feedback?"

When no one responded, he said, "We have another philosophy to consider, the focus on large accounts. I believe we should be the Lexus of our industry. Our volume of clients will be lower allowing us to provide individual attention."

He looked at Simon to see his reaction, and said, "I know, you have serious reservations."

"Yes, it makes me uncomfortable to think we won't have the avenue of smaller deals anymore. We have hundreds of smaller accounts now. Are we just going to turn them off?"

"Not overnight, but ultimately, yes," said Trent. "As we retool the company, we'll gear our focus, brand, and capabilities toward clients who engage us in a substantial manner. Choosing those clients will define who we are and what we do. That clarity will fuel our meaningful and sustained growth."

"While I struggle with it, it could work if we execute well," said Simon. "Speaking about execution, we've hired new salespeople who are volume generators. They're not experienced to sell client-centric services."

Trent sighed. "Hiring those salespeople without going through this corporate soul searching process was a mistake. We need salespeople who can engage executives in a substantive discussion as opposed to salespeople who are good at pushing a technology product to IT managers."

Simon lifted his thumbs and said, "There's a lot of risk involved in retooling, we ought to be careful."

"We could fail, but the risk of failure should not keep us from trying," said Trent. "I'll admit I'm nervous. Let's work together to make sure this retooling is a success."

Trent's Notes

Cohegic Method Takeaways

1. Great companies carefully select core management philosophies, and stick to them. Core philosophies define your company's business approach, eliminating potential confusion and distraction during strategy formulation, competency development, and business execution.

2. Unlike strategies, you do not change core management philosophies unless your company is reinventing itself in a major way. Because core philosophies color every aspect of your business from its culture to its competencies, changing philosophies is excruciating.

3. Identifying philosophies is only the beginning. Having the discipline to stick to them is the critical success factor. A leader must have the wherewithal to enforce discipline.

Trent's Notes

Hintec's Core Management Philosophies

Client-Centric Business Model

We will take the time to understand the needs of every one of our clients and deliver a specific business-intelligence solution that helps our clients achieve their business imperatives.

Focus on Upper-tier Accounts

We are an upper-tier business-intelligence solution provider. We work with clients who engage us in a significant manner. Our focus on the upper-tier allows us to deliver superior and customized client-specific solutions.

Chapter 8: Values

"It's raining heavily, why don't you skip today?" Lori asked as Trent grabbed an umbrella.

"It's already August, I better keep up the momentum." When Trent rang the bell, Watson let him in and quickly closed the door behind him. "Are you wet?"

"No, I'm okay. It's raining cats and dogs."

Martha took the umbrella to the kitchen to dry and the men took their seats in Watson's office.

Watson started, "By crystallizing the passion and the core philosophies you've articulated why Hintec exists and its business approach. Now you must describe how internal stakeholders must conduct themselves by crystallizing the organizational attitude and the mindset. Values, the third component of spirit, are a critical part of the foundation. They form the contract people have with each other."

"By values you mean team-work, excellence, etc."

"Yes." Watson could tell Trent didn't seem interested. "Not all companies take their values seriously, but values aren't fluff," he counseled. To drive his point, he reminded Trent, "Values drove Oscar's decision to let Maxell go and helped him convince the team about the decision's validity."

"Maxell did act unprofessionally," reflected Trent.

"Values can make or break a company."

"Isn't it a stretch to say that?"

"No. I'll share examples. Southwest Airlines' value is to focus on employees first. An employee focus isn't lip service, it embeds in their psyche."

"It's legendary," agreed Trent.

"Enron, Tyco, WorldCom, and Computer Associates paid the price of violating values. The misconduct of a few executives destroyed these companies. Some executives violate values, mistakenly considering it a sign of virility."

"Didn't Enron have honesty and excellence as values?"

"Sure did," replied Watson, "but the executives involved in the fraudulent schemes sought financial excellence at the cost of honesty. Articulating the values and describing their order of importance can help executives and employees make the right decisions during difficult and ambiguous situations."

"Those executives," argued Trent, "would have committed fraud regardless of what their values stated."

"Enron emphasized financial performance more heavily than honesty. Had Enron's management and board emphasized honesty and integrity more, it would have had a tempering effect on the culture of performance at any cost."

"The real issue is where to draw the line. What does honesty mean in gray areas?" commented Trent.

"That's precisely the guideline values should provide."

The next day as Trent returned to his office from a meeting, his assistant said, "Cedric returned your call."

"Thanks, Amy," he said. He went into his office and dialed the Chairman's number. Cedric answered.

"I looked into Clay Armstrong," said Trent. "He will make an excellent addition to Hintec's board."

"I already asked him," said Cedric. "He can't do it since he's serving on three other boards. I wish he had been available, it would have been good for you."

Trent paused. He struggled a little bit and said, "Cedric, as you know, I have an advisor. He's really helping me manage and lead coherently. I'm very happy with him."

"I'm glad to hear that, but don't underestimate what it requires to take an organization to a new level of growth."

"I won't," said Trent. "I appreciate your concern."

"Speaking about concerns, some of the board members have expressed concern our costs are high. Specifically, the operations in India seem to have a high run-rate over the last two quarters."

Trent hesitated. "It's not a high run-rate. I think those are one time charges that inflated their expenses."

"Look into it. Make sure our costs are in control, and let me know as soon as you find out."

"I will," said Trent sensing the urgency in Cedric's voice.

"I was looking to reduce my involvement in Hintec, and now I'm being dragged back into it," complained Cedric.

Trent thought long and hard after he put the phone down. Then he picked up the phone and called the CFO. She was not at her desk, so he left her a voice mail, "Fran, I need the detailed expense numbers on our Indian operations."

On Sunday evening, as he put on his sneakers, he told Lori, "I'm going to the park; I need to clear my head."

Watson was in his front yard gardening when he saw Trent walking past. "Where are you off to," he asked.

"The park. I need to unwind a little."

"Is everything okay?"

"Would you like to join me?" asked Trent.

"Sure, give me a minute to put my gardening tools away."

Once they reached the park, they sat down on a bench under a large oak. Seeing Trent's pensive look, Watson asked, "How're you feeling?"

"I'm anxious. I worry about how we'll implement all of this. I must produce success... fast."

Watson assured him calmly, "Worrying about the results causes anxiety. There's a saying, winning is everything, but if all you think about is winning, you stop focusing on playing."

"I know... if you keep looking at the score, you'll stop looking at the ball. But...."

"Only your effort," interjected Watson, "is under your control, not the outcome. Globez had a big office in Bangalore. While stationed there, I learned a saying, "Do your actions. Don't worry about the fruits of your actions.""

"How is it possible not to worry about the results?"

"Focus on your efforts instead of obsessing about the results. Obsessing is the key word here. Work toward achieving the best outcome but don't let thoughts about the outcome consume you."

"I don't... I don't want to fail."

"If your mind spends all its time worrying, your anxiety will undermine your ability to make things happen. Focus 80% on the effort and 20% on the outcome, instead of the other way around."

Trent looked down. Watson gave him a few moments, and then asked, "Are you doing your recliner exercises?"

Trent looked up. "I haven't been regular."

Watson looked squarely at him. "You'll receive no benefits if you aren't regular. What was your experience when you did?"

"A rush of thoughts, my mind races at a hundred miles an hour. It's boring to force yourself to sit down."

Watson looked straight ahead. "In today's world, we're over-stimulated with interruptions. We've lost the art of being peaceful. Doing this exercise regularly will lower your tension."

"But being tense keeps me vigilant, gives me an edge."

"Being tense before major events and during drastic situations makes sense, it's our natural instinct. Being tense all the time is a curse."

Trent nodded. "These changes are overwhelming."

"This method's coherent. The pieces will connect."

"I have confidence in your method, but you're not an expert in our industry."

"So, that's the real issue, my lack of industry knowledge," said Watson. "Another advisor with business-intelligence industry experience may advise different philosophies. I don't mind if you'd like to get a second opinion."

"No, that's all right," said Trent.

After dinner, Trent sat on the recliner in the master bedroom letting his mind process his thoughts. Then he joined Lori in the game room to watch TV.

On Monday morning, Trent went to see the CFO.

"Do you have the report on the Indian expenses?" he asked, standing by the door.

Fran looked up. "No. I've been consumed with the mid-year commission report and the monthly closing."

"I need it soon."

"Okay."

The next management meeting included another group of ten employees. Trent started, "Any feedback on our last meeting where we discussed the focus on large accounts?"

"I discussed that philosophy with my team that focuses on the Tier 3 calls," said Venkat. "They endorsed the philosophy and felt they'd be able to address the Tier 3 issues in the right manner because they'd be able to justify the time needed."

Trent nodded. "Thanks, Venkat." He looked around. "More feedback?" He paused, and then said, "Okay, today, our agenda is to identify our values. What should be our values?"

"Be professional," said the VP of HR.

"Can you elaborate," asked Hector.

"Be professional in our dealings with each other; conduct ourselves in a manner befitting a professional environment," elaborated Oscar.

Everyone nodded in agreement.

"I propose transparency," said Fran. "We should be transparent with our financials and how we make decisions. It'll create trust, and allow employees to have a better buy-in."

"I like transparency," seconded Hector.

"Teamwork," said an employee. "We should act as one team. Our different departments don't work well with each other."

"Very good suggestion," said Trent.

"We should strive to be the best," said Venkat. "We're a software company and we should produce the best software."

"I like that," said an employee. "We need to encourage the mind-set of product excellence within Hintec."

Oscar spoke, "Our philosophy is client-centric and delivering the best solution. Maybe we should call the fourth value, solution excellence as opposed to product excellence. Venkat, what do you think?"

"I agree," said Venkat.

Trent nodded. "That's good. Based on our discussion, Hintec's values, in order of importance, are professionalism, teamwork, transparency, and solution excellence."

"Would you explain the reasoning behind the ordering?" asked an employee.

"Sure. Professionalism is the most important. Unless we act professionally, we can't achieve teamwork. Teamwork is next. Without teamwork, we hurt ourselves by not cooperating, and can cease to function as a company. Is this making sense?"

Several people nodded.

"Transparency is third because it's about good governance. It increases investor, employee, and customer confidence. Having the first three values incorporated in Hintec's psyche will help us achieve solution excellence."

Another employee spoke, "These values make sense to me, and I appreciate the order of importance. It tells me, how my coworkers and I behave with each other is the most important. If we are professional with each other, the rest will follow."

"Absolutely. It is the basic building block," said Trent. He stopped and looked around the table. "I'm glad we've adopted these values. They're important, and I promise I'll ask myself if I'm adhering to them."

"We all will," offered Oscar. "That's a good list." Several employees nodded.

Before leaving that evening, Trent went to see Fran. "Do you have the report on the Indian expenses?"

She gestured him to take a seat. "I know you want the report soon. I contacted the Indian office and asked for a complete and detailed report on all their expenses. I'm waiting on them."

"Why's it taking so darn long?" said Trent, irritated.

"I'll call them again tomorrow. They're closed now," said Fran. "I've been consumed. Two of my team members have been out for the last two weeks."

Trent's face turned red.

"You're the CFO. I expect you to make it happen, not make excuses. That report is critical and I needed it yesterday."

"I am making it happen," she said giving him a stern look. "They are in a different time zone."

"I have so much faith in you, and you can't even produce a simple report. Can you get me the report ASAP?"

Fran frowned. "I'll call them again tonight from home."

That evening, when he met Watson, Trent said, "Lori asked me to invite you and Martha over for a casual dinner tomorrow."

"Are you sure? Lori's probably still recovering."

"It was her idea. She's going to order food in."

Watson hesitated.

"We'd really like for you both to come over."

"Okay. I'll check with Martha, but I'm sure it'll be okay."

"Our session on values went well, and I received an email with positive feedback from one of the employees."

He gave Watson a sheet with Hintec's values.

"Good work. Share them with the board and all the employees for feedback. Ask your team to develop a detailed description for each value. Answer questions such as, how should employees act professionally when a client is abusive? What's Hintec's stand in such situations?"

"That's adding a lot of bureaucracy."

"You don't have to go overboard by writing a thesis. But by addressing the questions now, the employees will know the right approach to handle urgent or difficult situations."

"Is there any value we've missed?"

"There's a value that matters a lot to me. It's sort of covered by professionalism and teamwork."

"Which one?"

"Respect," answered Watson. "Respect is critical for building a long-lasting organization. Without it, you'll lose talent."

"But you can't be nice to everyone all the time. You have to let people know when they're failing. There has to be accountability."

"Respect doesn't imply underperformance. Respect isn't about what you ask, but how you ask it. You can provide critical feedback, but you must provide it constructively."

Trent struggled. "I'm not sure I know how."

"What do you want to accomplish? Do you want to chastise the person or do you want a different result?"

"I want a different result."

"Good, then make the feedback not be about the person but about what you want. That would allow the other person to try harder or try a different approach, giving them a second chance. If they feel indicted, they'll feel there's nothing they can do rectify the situation."

Trent closed his eyes in thought.

"In many situations, the problem is you don't communicate the request properly or don't allow the other person enough time to understand it. Giving feedback should be about clarifying the request and understanding what went wrong."

Watson stopped and waited.

Trent nodded. "I'm digesting what you're saying. I struggle with the words to use to provide non-personal feedback."

"Okay. Share an example of a situation."

"Recently, I asked Fran to get me a report. When in spite of reminders, I didn't receive it I went to see her. I told her, I needed the report and it was beyond me why she hadn't delivered it!"

"What was her reaction?"

"She was defensive and made excuses, which upset me."

"Why was this report so important and urgent?"

"Cedric said the board members had raised questions about the Indian expenses. I needed the detailed itemized expense report to show we have a low cost structure."

"Did you tell Fran why it was important and urgent to you?"

"No."

"Did you finally get the report?"

"Not yet," said Trent, remembering he still needed it badly.

"What could you have done differently?" asked Watson, pressing him.

Trent thought about it. "I could've told her right away why the report was urgent."

"What could you have told her about the priority of the report versus the other things on her plate?"

"It was higher than anything else she was working on."

"Did you need ballpark numbers or precise information?"

"That's a good point. I could've told her all I needed urgently were ballpark numbers. She could take the time later to produce a more detailed report."

"See, there you have it."

Trent smiled. "Adopting values in a meeting and committing to adhere to them is one thing. Really understanding how you have to change personally to inculcate the values is another. Thank you," he said emphatically.

Watson nodded knowingly. "By defining the mission, core philosophies and values, you have crystallized the foundation. Now you're ready to define Hintec's future direction."

"I hope the team's discussion on direction will be more structured than in the past."

"Keep at it. Slowly and surely, the team will begin to appreciate the logical and systematic approach to thinking through all of Hintec's critical business aspects."

Returning home, Trent told Lori that Watson and Martha would come for dinner. Then he said, "I've learned the right way to provide feedback. Hopefully, this will allow me to say what I need to say without offending others."

Lori smiled as she rocked Catherine.

Trent did the recliner exercise before going to bed.

The next morning, Trent went to see Fran. After sitting down, he said, "I didn't communicate effectively about the report on the Indian expenses."

She looked at him, not sure what to expect.

"I need ballpark numbers to share with the board. They're concerned our Indian run-rate is up in the last two quarters."

"Ah," said Fran. "I was waiting for the latest detailed breakdown, but I can answer the board's concern. The Indian run-rate isn't up. It looks so because they provide us total expenses, which combines capital and operational expenses, and we report the total to the board. They've had capital expenditures in the last two quarters, which they received approval for."

"I thought it was capital expenditure, and I told that to Cedric, but I wasn't sure."

Fran swung back towards her computer.

"I have the capital expenditure approval with me. I can look up the numbers for you."

"You're a life saver."

She turned around. "I better revel in the moment because I know it can change fast," she said, and smiled as she pushed her hair behind her ear.

Cedric was in the office. Trent ran into him as he walked back from Fran's office. They went to Trent's office. Once they sat down, Trent shared, "Fran has figured out the Indian run-rate is within the budget. The expenses were one-time charges."

Cedric nodded. "Stay on top of costs."

"We will," said Trent. "Here's a copy of the values we finalized yesterday." He gave Cedric a sheet with the values and another with the mission and philosophies.

Without looking at them, Cedric asked, "How're sales?"

"Third quarter numbers will beat the second quarter, but they won't reach $35 million. I realize now, $35 million was an unrealistic goal. I was eyeing 20% revenue growth, and $35 million in new sales every quarter was the road to it."

"Are we going to grow this year?" asked Cedric, his eyes piercing Trent.

"In the single digits...."

Cedric pushed the sheets of paper around. Trent waited for him to respond, but when Cedric didn't, Trent offered, "Once we implement our new philosophies, we'll dramatically improve our client retention rate and supercharge our sales. I'm confident we're on the path to meaningful and sustained growth."

Cedric glanced over the sheets and asked, "How're things going with implementing Watson's method."

Pointing to the sheets, Trent replied, "As you can see, we're making great progress."

Cedric took a few minutes to read the sheets. "I like the direction in which you're headed. As I told you last week, I like the mission and philosophies you've developed. I'll study the values. They may need more elaboration."

"I agree. We'll elaborate them further, and then add them to the employee handbook."

As he got up to leave, Cedric said, "There is very little room for error. Make sure you don't take your eye off the ball."

Trent's Notes

Cohegic Method Takeaways

1. Values have the power to make or break an organization. An important part of spirit, values define the behavioral contract between people.

2. Values can compete with each other. For instance, honesty and financial excellence, in certain situations, can be competing values. Order the values, so it is clear which values are more important.

3. Explain the values in detail. For example, management must provide detailed guidelines on how employees and management must face difficult situations beforehand, so people do not lose their bearings. And, no, people won't act with "common sense" in trying times, unless they have been trained and instructed to do so.

Leadership and Personal Takeaways

1. Respect is not about what you say, but how you say it.

2. Communicate clearly, and ensure the other person understands your direction.

3. Follow-through not to chastise but to clarify the request further, understand what is working, and what is not.

4. As a leader, you must really understand how you have to change personally in order to imbibe the values.

5. Do your actions. Don't worry about the fruits of your action. Focus 80% on the effort and 20% on the outcome, instead of the other way around.

Trent's Notes

Hintec's Values

Professionalism

We expect professional conduct that includes respect and courtesy for co-workers. We promise to interact with our vendors, customers, and investors in a professional manner and expect the same in return.

Teamwork

Houmatics stresses collective success — we succeed as a company, not as individual departments. We expect collaboration across and within departments.

Transparency

Transparent decision-making is critical to earn the trust of our co-workers. We will be as transparent as we can without compromising competitive advantage. Transparency is about openness and inclusion. We encourage open, frank and polite communication.

Solution Excellence

We are committed to excellence. We will relentlessly strive to provide the best solution for our clients.

Section 4: Direction

Chapters in the Direction section:

Chapter 9: Vision

Chapter 10: Goals

Chapter 11: Strategies

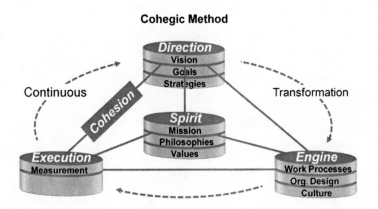

Chapter 9: Vision

When Watson and Martha came for dinner, Ethan answered the door. Martha handed him a gift. Ethan tore open the wrapping. "It's a book on trains," he exclaimed.

"Say, thank you," said Trent. Ethan did.

Lori came from the kitchen to welcome them. "Dinner's on the table," she said. "I'm glad you like Chinese food. It's our favorite." They ate dinner chatting about everyday matters and finished with an ice-cream cake.

After dessert, while Trent helped clear the table, Watson walked out to the flagstone patio. When Trent came out, Watson was standing at the edge of the swimming pool. "I was admiring your vanishing edge pool," said Watson, walking back to the patio. "The water flowing over the far edge makes the pool seem to flow into the lake."

"Thanks. Lori chose the infinity pool design. It's one of the reasons we love living in Houston. You can afford to live in a fabulous home."

Trent pulled together two wrought iron chairs. Watson started as soon as he sat down, "The first step towards creating a cohegic Hintec is to define the spirit, which you have done. Now, it's time for you to crystallize the next facet, direction."

"Where Hintec is headed?"

"That's right. Direction defines the destination and charts the road to it. While spirit articulates what the organization is about, direction describes what it's trying to achieve, the road it will follow and the speed. I divide direction into three levels: vision, goals, and strategies."

"I'd like to hear your definition of those terms. I come across so many different and confusing versions."

"Vision is the major thrust; goals are the markers to reach the vision; strategies are the approaches, the how each goal may be accomplished."

"And all of them are dynamic," commented Trent.

"Yes, while spirit is static, direction and all its components are dynamic. To define Hintec's direction, we'll start with the destination, the vision. It will describe the future Hintec desires, the picture on the horizon so to speak."

"How do you get everyone to agree on a common vision?"

"Ah, a great question. When the vision statement is overarching, you'll find it easier to build a consensus. If you discuss details prematurely, it'll be harder to build a consensus. Details belong in the discussions on goals and strategies. The vision statement is an energizing, big-picture statement."

"So while mission creates commitment, vision should create excitement."

"Very good!" Watson clapped his hands in applause.

Trent smiled. "What is your time-frame for the vision?"

"It depends on the organization. For Hintec, I'd develop a three-year vision. You may also develop a long-term vision but the three-year vision should be your priority."

"Okay."

Lori and Martha walked out. "Are we interrupting?" asked Lori.

"No, not at all," said Watson.

Trent pulled closer a couple of more chairs. The four chatted for sometime before the Hughes left for home.

"They're nice people," said Lori. "It was sweet of Martha to bring a book for Ethan."

"We should do something special for them," said Trent. "Watson's been very helpful. If Hintec had hired a consultant to do this, it would've cost a bit."

"Well, it goes beyond Hintec saving money."

Trent nodded. "Cedric's under a lot of pressure because of me. If I save my job it'll be because of Watson."

"Shouldn't you get Hintec to pay Watson?"

"I guess we could, but that might require Watson to come in to the office, which is something he doesn't want to do. I must think of another way to thank him."

Trent went to see the CFO the following day. When he knocked on her door, Fran looked up.

"Oh, oh, what did I do now?" she said and smiled.

"Nothing," he said with a smirk, as he took a seat.

"How can I help you?"

"Pricing. I spoke to two more clients and they too responded positively to the client-centric approach. The question is how should we charge?"

"Hmm... how should we charge and how much?" said Fran, as she pondered.

"Would you put that on your back-burner so you can be thinking about it? I don't want to charge an hourly fee for our resources. Hintec should not be seen as pushing consulting to generate more revenues."

Trent started the next meeting by addressing the employees, "Thanks for taking the time to join us. So far, we've developed our mission, philosophies, and values. I shared them with the board and received good feedback. I'll forward them to everyone in Hintec this week for feedback as well. I have copies for you here." He passed the sheets around and continued, "Our agenda today is to develop our three-year vision. Where would we like to be in three years?"

"I'll start it off," said Fran. "In three years we should be larger in terms of revenues. So our vision is growth."

"Why should growth be our vision?" asked the VP of customer service glaring at her.

Looking bewildered, Fran said, "How can it not be?"

"It doesn't have to be," pushed back Hector. "In the past years, we didn't waste money trying to grow revenues; we generated healthy profits and were quite happy. The board was happy too."

Trent winced, taken aback by Hector's strong and open push back. He quickly glanced at the faces of the employees, wondering how they might be viewing the proceedings.

The VP of HR stepped in, "But now, we have new board members who represent private equity firms that have invested in Hintec. They want to grow revenues; that's how they'll get a return on their investment. Hector, as an owner, you'll make more money too when Hintec increases in value."

"That could be wishful thinking," said Hector. "We're introducing significant changes and it's not clear we'll succeed. We should stick to what we know and make the most money doing it."

"You mean milk it," said Trent, not masking his annoyance.

"There's no shame in admitting it," retorted Hector. "The employees would like it too, they'll have bigger bonuses."

"I want to be part of a company that's growing," said Venkat calmly. "I want to grow in my career and skills. I want money, but I don't want to be in a stalemate."

The employees who'd been watching the proceedings nodded in agreement. Trent smiled at Venkat.

"The vision should be exciting," said Trent. "We're not here to preside over what we already have. We're here to make Hintec larger and better in three years. Growth isn't just about revenues; it's about rejuvenation. We must continuously transform Hintec." He looked at Hector. "You're right, we sacrifice short-term profitability for future revenues, but if we execute well, we'll generate more profits than we invest. I appreciate your point, but to keep the discussion progressing, let's move on."

Hector shrugged his shoulders.

Trent walked to the white board and wrote down vision and underneath it, he wrote, growth. Turning toward the group, he said, "That's the first component of our vision. What other aspects do we envision?

"I have one," said Oscar, "in three years, we should envision a Hintec that has upgraded its capabilities, processes and resources to become fully client-centric."

"Thanks, Oscar," said Trent as he wrote it down.

"Be recognized as a premier business-intelligence provider," offered Venkat.

"I love that. It fits with our value of solution excellence," said Trent. "Of course, to be recognized as such, first we have to become fully client-centric, deliver, and grow."

Venkat acknowledged with a nod.

"Other suggestions?" asked Trent. He waited, and then said, "Okay, we have a three-pronged vision: growth, become fully client-centric, and recognition."

"Client-centric is a philosophy and you mentioned it also as part of the vision. I'm confused," said an employee.

"Good question," said Trent. "Even though client-centric is our philosophy, we aren't there yet. Therefore, we have to list becoming client-centric as part of our three-year vision."

"Okay. Thanks," said the employee.

"Do we agree on our three-year vision?" asked Trent.

"Yes," said Fran, Oscar, and Venkat.

"I've also been thinking about our long-term vision," said Trent. "In ten years, we should have a sizeable share of the business-intelligence global market. We should be one of the top three."

Trent had set up a meeting with the Chairman.

"Come in," said Cedric when Trent knocked at his door.

Trent closed the door, sat down, and began, "Watson has been excellent. His advice is profound, and it's helping me piece everything together."

"I like your progress."

"Watson has never asked for any compensation, but I feel obligated. I need your advice on what Hintec can do for him to thank him for his advice and his method."

"Let me think about that," said Cedric. "...If the next board meeting goes well, I'll talk to the board members."

"Thanks, Cedric," said Trent tepidly.

"We had a good time at your place," said Watson, as he and Trent walked out to Watson's deck, that evening.

"We had a good time as well," said Trent. As they sat down, he added, "We developed a three-year vision with three components." He gave Watson a sheet with the vision.

After Watson read it, he said, "I like it. All the three vision components link back to your core philosophies. It's all about ensuring cohegic flow between the facets."

Trent nodded, and then turned dour. "I wish Simon and Hector would join the bandwagon. Simon didn't say a word during the meeting. And Hector still wants to milk the company for profit. I'm under so much pressure. It's frustrating that these guys disregard growth. They don't get it!" said Trent shaking his head.

"Is growth extremely important to you?"

"It'll save my job... growth gives me a sense of accomplishment. I'm thirsty for growth. I will be able to tell the board I accomplished what my predecessor couldn't."

Watson rubbed his chin.

"Watson, you've made me self-aware. I can see I'm being competitive, but I won't apologize for wanting to succeed."

Watson laughed. Trent frowned. "What's funny?"

"I have you scared of me."

"No," protested Trent. Then he shrugged and said, "Yes. I'm confused. I don't want you to tell me I should become calm and give up my passion for growth."

"I won't ever ask you to give up your passion, but I'll ask you to give up your obsession. Passion's a blessing, obsession's a curse, and there's a fine line. If you consume food in the right quantity it nourishes, otherwise it becomes a cause for disease."

"Obsession could be a source of strength," argued Trent.

"No. Obsession is always a source of weakness. The obsessed lose perspective and become fanatical."

Trent squirmed.

"I'm a believer in growth and you must pursue it, but in a well-managed manner. The danger of pursuing growth for the sake of growth is that you begin to want it at any cost. Push Hintec to grow as fast as it can, but no faster."

Trent looked puzzled.

"Don't push to a point where the pursuit is uncontrolled, becomes chaotic and tears the fabric. Cycle through the dynamic facets of direction, engine, and execution. And, in each cycle if you push to transform and evolve Hintec, you will produce growth naturally in all aspects."

"I agree with that."

"Let's talk about Simon and Hector. Why is Simon hanging back? Does his sales team have the desired skills set?"

"No, the sales team doesn't have the necessary skills. Simon likes the idea at the surface, but he hasn't digested it completely. I need to have a heart-to-heart talk with him."

"What about Hector?"

"Hector likes big bonuses. In the past, we rewarded profitability and not growth. I'll talk to Cedric. We should adjust the compensation scheme to pay people for producing growth. I wonder if that'll change his attitude."

"Try it. It's a good idea," approved Watson. "Next, you must rank your three vision components in importance on a scale of 1 to 10, 10 being max. The ranking exercise will clarify which components are the most important."

"Understood," said Trent. "Along with our three-year vision, I put forth a ten-year vision to become one of the top three players in the global market. Is that outlandish?"

"Ten years is a long time. Achieving your mid-term vision may allow you to pursue your long-term vision aggressively. The question now to answer is how Hintec will generate growth with its new high-touch, client-centric philosophy? It's the million dollar question that your strategies and the selection of your goals should answer, which is our agenda for next time."

"It's the $350 million question. With 20% annual growth, that's how large we need to be at the end of three years." The earlier discussion still bothering him, Trent asked, "How do you tell obsession from passion?"

Watson smiled, knowing he had touched a nerve. "When you obsess, you stop listening, judge others, and find ways to silence those who disagree with you. When you're passionate, you listen well. If things don't go your way, you regroup and continue to apply yourself."

"I'm passionate, not obsessed," asserted Trent.

"We'll go with that. I have no obsession to prove you're obsessed," said Watson and laughed.

Trent smiled too.

"Am I obsessed?" Trent asked Lori, as she watched TV in the upstairs game room.

She turned towards him. "Obsessed with what?"

"Obsessed with work and career?"

She raised her eyebrows and smiled wryly.

"Aw, come on," he protested. "I'm not obsessed." He wiggled his shoulders and said, "I'm passionate."

"Whatever you say honey," she said and hugged him.

"I'm going to do my recliner exercises," he said and walked downstairs to go to the master bedroom.

The next day Fran stopped by Trent's office.

"I came to discuss the client-centric pricing."

"Sure, what did you come up with?"

"We charge 15% for annual support and maintenance." As she widened her eyes, she said, "Maybe we increase it to 21% and include client-centric services. Also, we can increase our initial setup fees to include the up-front work that is needed to incorporate a business-intelligence solution."

"I like that. Would you look at the range from 16% to 23%, so we get a complete idea?"

"Okay, I'll work on the numbers and create projections."

"Once you do that, I'll go back to the clients I've talked to and get their feedback on our pricing approach."

After Fran left, Trent picked up the phone and called the Chairman. Cedric answered. After exchanging pleasantries, Trent said, "We need to adjust the management team's compensation scheme to reward growth."

"I recognize that," said Cedric. "One of the reasons why Barry chose to focus on profitability was because we weren't rewarding him to produce growth."

"Do we need the board's permission to make changes?"

"It'll be ill-timed for me to approach them to make any changes to your compensation scheme. But you have the authority to put new guidelines in for your team. I'll support your new compensation incentives."

"Thanks. This will go a long way in aligning the team."

Trent visited with Simon and spent some time trying to get the VP of sales excited about the new philosophies and direction, but Trent was not nearly as satisfied with the conversation as he would have liked.

Oscar stopped by Trent's office at the end of the day.

"It's been over four weeks since we let Maxell go. What're your thoughts on filling the VP marketing role? The marketing team is without a leader."

"Let's see what goals and strategies we develop. I don't want to repeat the mistake of hiring someone and then finding out I'm out-of-sync with them on the direction."

"But the direction could change."

"Sure. But having a better handle on the direction will tell us what skills, experience and temperament we should look for. It improves our chances of being on the same page."

"Okay, sounds good," said Oscar, agreeing with Trent.

In the next meeting, Trent shared that the compensation scheme for the management team will be revisited and adjusted to reward growth. He waited for Hector's reaction.

"I still haven't bought the notion of chasing growth," said Hector. "But at least you're being consistent, by changing the compensation to align with your vision."

"Good point. The compensation scheme will be consistent and coherent not just with growth, but with all the visions, goals and strategies we develop. We'll finalize the scheme in the execution phase."

He looked at his watch. "Oh, I better ask Amy to send in the group of employees waiting to join us."

After he brought the employees up to speed, Trent said, "Now that we've developed our vision, let's rank the relative importance of the three components. Let me suggest some numbers." He walked to the board, and wrote, "Growth – 10; become fully client-centric – 10; Recognition – 7."

"I'm not so sure," said Venkat. "Recognition is more important than growth. We should rank it the highest."

Trent thought about it. "I see what you're saying, but achieving growth is the most important. It'd be perfectly okay if we grew but weren't yet recognized as a premier BI supplier."

"Well…," murmured Venkat.

"Actually, becoming client-centric is the most important," said Oscar. "If we didn't grow it'd be okay, but client-centric we must become."

Trent squirmed, "Growth's important to me… and the board."

"Growth is important," said Fran, "but, first, it's far more important for Hintec to be reborn as client-centric."

"It's interesting to see you all buy into client-centric to such a great deal," said Trent. "Growing is important, yet I can't argue that client-centric shouldn't be more important."

He wrote on the board, saying, "Client-centric is now a 10, growth is an 8 and premier recognition is a 7."

He stepped back and said, "I'm a little bit concerned how the board will react. I guess we're not saying growing isn't important, we'll still pursue it vigorously."

"Yes, we will," said Fran. "I'm glad we ranked the vision components. You, Venkat and Oscar have your preferences and I can see why. These rankings increased our clarity."

"I'm with you," said Oscar. "Ranking the vision components has increased transparency, one of our values."

"You're right," agreed Trent. "Now, our challenge is to develop the right goal and strategies to realize this vision."

Trent's Notes

Cohegic Method Takeaways

1. Companies often confuse mission and vision, but there is a big difference. Mission is the eternal purpose, while vision is the desired state at a given point in the future. While mission rarely changes, vision changes once the organization achieves it. Mission should create commitment, while vision should create excitement.

2. Management members are likely to have their personal favorite vision component. Therefore, the management team must rank all the vision components to clarify which are more important, and agree on the ranking.

3. Vision must be in-sync with the organization's spirit — cohegic flow.

Leadership and Personal Takeaways

1. A leader must have passion, not obsession. It is a fine line. When a leader is blindly in love with him/herself, his/her company or product, that's when he or she begins to make big mistakes.

2. Sometimes, leaders obsess with producing growth, wanting it at any cost. A leader must pursue growth in a well-managed manner without tearing the core fabric. If an organization cycles through the dynamic facets of direction, engine, and execution, and in each cycle transforms and evolves itself, it will produce growth naturally, and at the right pace.

Trent's Notes

Hintec's Vision

Long-term Vision (7 to 10 years)

Be one of the top three companies in the business-intelligence marketplace and have a sizeable market-share of the global market.

Three-Year Vision

- Client-centric Vision (10): Fulfill our philosophy of being client-centric. Our thrust is to build our client-centric capabilities, augment our business-intelligence delivery resources, and successfully deliver our services.

- Growth Vision (8): Achieve significant growth in the upper-tier of the marketplace — growth in revenues, significance, and size of client engagements. Growth will create greater value for our clients and provide career development opportunities for our co-workers and superior financial returns for our investors.

- Recognition Vision (7): Gain recognition as a premier upper-tier business-intelligence service provider that's the best in helping clients make superior business-decisions.

Chapter 10: Goals

When Trent rang Watson's doorbell it was a few minutes before Watson opened. "Sorry, we were in the middle of dinner. Martha has baked a wonderful pecan pie. Come have a slice."

Trent joined them at the table and ate a slice. He thanked Martha and then the men walked out to the deck.

Once they sat down, Watson began, "By articulating your three and ten-year visions, you've set the stage, defined the thrust and direction in which Hintec is headed."

"We do know where we want to be in three years."

"Next, break down your vision into manageable chunks by defining the markers Hintec must achieve on the way to realizing the vision. I'm talking about goals, the second part of direction. The choice of your goals will reveal to the rest of Hintec how you propose to achieve the vision."

"That is a good point. Our goals have typically existed in a vacuum. Now we'll be tying them back to our vision... cohegic flow."

"I'm glad you like the idea of cohegic flow so much," said Watson, teasing Trent. Trent smiled.

Watson continued, "Develop a batch of goals for the first year. After you accomplish them, a batch for the second year, and finally a batch for the third year. Your goals must come together like a well-fit puzzle. Goals have a cause and effect relationship. For example, improving customer experience is a cause that affects improving financial results."

"I recognize that."

"And, remember to rank the goals."

"Absolutely," said Trent. "Ranking the vision components was quite insightful for us."

"Good. When you don't communicate which are more important, goals compete for mind share and resources."

"I suspect these rankings are dynamic so you would adjust them to reflect changing conditions."

"Exactly," beamed Watson, "by changing the relative importance, you'll signal to Hintec the new adjusted thrust in a coherent manner."

"Understood," said Trent. "Do you advocate SMART goals: specific, measureable, achievable, results oriented, and time-based?"

"Yes. When we discuss execution, we'll define the metrics and targets, so each goal will have the SMART attributes."

The next morning, Trent stopped by his assistant's cubicle.

"Can you set up more management meetings?" he asked.

"I'm getting pushback from the other admins," Amy replied in a low voice. "Some management team members are complaining about the volume of meetings."

Trent thought about it.

"A break might be good," suggested Amy.

"I'll think about it… I'd hate to lose momentum."

Simon knocked on Trent's door a few minutes later. Trent invited him to take a seat.

"I just heard from the CIO of NAPIT Oil," shared the VP of sales. "They've decided to go with GenceSoft."

Trent frowned. "Did you remind Kathy we helped them develop their needs?"

"I did, she apologized. Because she felt a little guilty she shared some insights into what GenceSoft is doing."

Trent's ears perked up.

"To acquire market share they're selling stripped down versions of their modules including the business-intelligence module at half the price. Kathy realizes they focus on different things, while we focus only on BI. She agrees our BI offering is better, but couldn't pass up the opportunity."

"Why is GenceSoft so desperate?" said Trent, as he pondered. "They're much larger than us, and do deals that are at least ten to fifteen times our average deal."

"I hear their CEO is under pressure to compete with the other big players," shared Simon.

"How should we respond?" mulled Trent.

"Match their price?" suggested Simon.

"Then we can kiss our quarterly sales goal goodbye. The board will roast me alive. This is serious. Let's call the team."

Venkat and Fran were the only ones available. Trent asked them to come to his office. After Trent explained the situation, the VP of engineering said, "Our design is modular. It won't be difficult to create a limited-features version of our software."

"Great," said Simon. "We can offer the limited-version at a lower price."

Trent looked unsure.

"If we do that, are we playing by GenceSoft's rules?" asked the CFO. "How can we reframe the situation?"

"Good point, Fran," said Trent. "GenceSoft is focused on large-scale corporate data integration with BI as only one of the modules on top, while we focus only on BI. We should find an answer that fits our philosophies and direction."

Simon looked perplexed, and dismayed. Trent got up and looked out the window, deep in thought. "What are our philosophies?" he asked turning around.

"Client-centric and focus on upper-tier," replied Venkat.

"That's right," said Trent. "If we were product-centric, we would be responding to GenceSoft's price war. All the other players in the space will do just that until better sense prevails. If we match the price cut, we won't be able to sustain our client-centric approach. We must differentiate based on our philosophies and demand a premium instead."

"But, we're not client-centric yet," argued Simon. "It will take time, by then we might be finished."

"That's a dramatic statement," said Trent shaking his head dismissively. "We need the discipline to not abandon our philosophy in difficult situations. NAPIT chose GenceSoft because they don't know about our client-centric approach. We must work it into our sales message."

Fran looked at Trent. "From what you've told me, most of our customers you've talked to like the client-centric approach. Becoming client-centric will allow us to retain existing customers, and tide over this price war."

"Simon, Fran is right," said Trent. "GenceSoft can't keep this up for long. Let's watch closely how their pricing war plays out and how it'll affect us. As far as I can tell, we're competing with them in very few deals. Is that right?"

Simon shrugged his shoulders. "It's difficult to find out how many of our deals they're a factor in because prospects are reluctant to share that information."

Trent looked at him intently.

"But I'll continue to find out," said Simon to placate Trent.

"We should visit with Kathy and see if we can still work with her," said Trent. "Can you set up a meeting?"

"I'll try," said Simon. "She may not be too keen to meet us with right now."

"Try. If not now, then in a few weeks."

Trent opened the next meeting, "Today our agenda is to develop our twelve-month goals that will put us on the path to achieving our three-year vision."

"We have goals for this calendar year. Are we going to replace them?" asked Simon.

"We only set sales related goals. Let's see where today's discussion takes us," Trent responded. Turning to the others, he said, "What should be our twelve-month goals to achieve our top ranked vision, becoming fully client-centric?"

"Develop business-intelligence delivery resources," suggested the VP of HR. "We need experienced resources who can work with our client organizations and their senior management."

"That's a critical skill," said Trent, writing down the resources goal on the white board. "More goals?"

"I have one, build standard delivery processes," said the CFO. "We need to ensure consistent and high quality delivery."

"Great suggestion," said Trent.

"I have one more," said Fran as she smiled. "Should we have an industry-specific focus?"

"Another, great suggestion," said Trent. "If we focus on a few industry verticals, we'll become even more client-centric. We can hire resources and create processes specific to those industries."

Fran nodded.

"What other goals under the vision component, become fully client-centric?" asked Trent. There were no other suggestions. "Okay, now let's tackle the next ranked, growth vision. What goals should we define underneath it?"

As soon as he asked the question, he said, "I know, improve sales effectiveness."

"How much growth should we aim for?" asked Fran.

"20% annual growth in revenues would make the board happy," said Trent. "If we achieve that, in three years we'll be at $350 million."

"What's our strategy?" asked Hector. "Do we even have a prayer of achieving 20% growth?"

Trent answered calmly, "We'll discuss strategy once we identify all the goals. But your point is well made; I fully realize achieving 20% growth is an extremely huge challenge, but maybe our new approach will give us a better chance."

"What about improving customer retention?" asked Fran.

"Absolutely," said Trent. "It's one of our foremost goals."

"How're we going to do that?" asked Hector.

"Again, we'll figure out the how when we discuss strategy," responded Trent. He tapped his pen on the table a few times, and said, "Hector, I sense resistance. What's on your mind? Do you feel we're going in the wrong direction?"

"The direction's right," replied Hector. "But I'm not convinced we're going to do anything with these goals. I know a lot of companies that spend time coming up with goals, mission and vision, and then nothing happens."

Trent nodded. "If we don't implement what we develop, we would've wasted our time. This method is different. It's logical. It flows from one facet to the next. If you all work with me, we'll produce results, I promise."

"This method is systematic," emphasized Oscar. "Our discussions have made progress, as opposed to some of our other meetings where we've gone in circles."

Trent acknowledged and asked, "Other goals?"

"What about adding product features? Is that still a goal?" asked the VP of engineering.

Trent smiled. "Until now, I had pushed for bells and whistles. From now on, we'll focus on functional features that'll make it easier for customers to adopt BI."

Venkat grinned broadly.

Trent looked at him and smiled too.

Simon looked flustered. "We're making a u-turn. Those features help us sell. Sizzle is at least as important as the steak."

Trent replied calmly, "We made a u-turn when we chose client-centric as our philosophy. What we're doing now is ensuring our goals and product decisions are consistent with our philosophy. We're becoming a different company."

Fran asked, "What does a premier business-intelligence provider mean? If it's not product leadership, what is it?"

"I love your question," said Trent. "It gives us an opportunity to understand the shift we've made. We don't aspire to be the premier BI provider based on our product, but based on our overall solution. We don't want software magazines to rank us based on most features, biggest computational engine, and technical features. We want business magazines to rank us the best because we provide clients the most help in making better decisions. Product alone is no longer our focus. How we leverage it to make a difference for our clients is the focus. That's our transformation."

That evening as Trent walked into the kitchen from the garage, Lori asked, "How was your day?"

"Good," he said.

Ethan ran up and jumped into Trent's arms. Trent carried him into the game room, and played with him and Catherine until dinner was on the table. Lori had prepared Mexican quesadillas. "Oh, yum," said Trent, and Ethan clapped his hands.

"We had an epiphany in our meeting today," said Trent, as he helped clear the table after they finished dinner. "We've clearly realized our product isn't our focus; how we use the product to help our customers is our focus."

"I could've told you that," said Lori widening her eyes.

"Of course, honey," said Trent, "but, you know me, I wouldn't have listened to you, even if you had."

"Now that's the truth," she said and smiled.

He poked her in the side and they both laughed.

Trent drew a goal hierarchy chart that linked the goals to the vision components and showed it to Watson.

Looking at the chart, Watson said, "I can see where Hintec is headed. I like that your vision and goals are tightly integrated."

Trent smiled.

Watson continued, "I hope you realize the path you've set through your choice of goals."

"No, I didn't," said Trent, perplexed.

"Your goals are geared toward internal improvements."

"That makes sense for us. We were confused about our philosophies. So first, we must focus on reorienting internally, and then, develop a new vision for market penetration."

"Okay," said Watson.

"Should we make the goals specific? For instance, specify client retention must increase 90%?"

"We will add specifics when we develop metrics and targets in the execution discussion."

"Okay," said Trent. "Changing subjects, I have a concern. The management team's been spending a lot of time. I'm beginning to hear rumblings. Also, I'm getting questions about when we're going to start implementing these decisions."

"Typically, companies take months to go through what you've accomplished in a matter of weeks. You need to be ready to go into the next board meeting and show them a different CEO by presenting a cohegic Hintec."

"I do need them to appreciate what we've developed here."

"Hintec will do much better when it heads in this new direction. Change management is difficult, and the longer it takes, the lower the success rate. Tell your team members and the board, you need to keep pressing on."

Trent called the Chairman the next morning,

"Cedric, this is Trent. Is this a good time for you to talk?"

"Sure."

"As you know, we're making fantastic progress. We now have the vision and the twelve-month goals defined. I'll email those to you. Next, we'll tackle strategy."

"Good progress."

"We're going through the process as fast as we can, but it's taking time. It's the right thing to do..."

"I know," Cedric interrupted. "This initiative is important, I wish you had done it when you started as CEO, but better late than never. I hear the complaints, but I'm with you. To break out of our flat growth quagmire we must rethink, and move fast. We can't repeat the same things and expect different results."

"Thank you, Cedric. I appreciate your encouragement and confidence. I shared the mission, values and philosophies with all the employees via email. Their feedback was very positive."

"Good work. Continue your progress."

Trent hesitated. "...Will the board respond favorably to the progress we're making?"

Cedric was silent. Then he said, "I don't know. But don't let that stop you. Focus on making progress quickly and we'll see how the next board meeting plays out."

That afternoon, Trent told the management team, "We've spent considerable time in these meetings but we must keep pushing. If you have pressing matters, skip a meeting, but do your best to attend them all. We need your ideas, and more importantly, we need your intrinsic and enthusiastic buy-in."

"We realize this exercise is important," said the CFO, "and, the right thing for Hintec."

"Thanks, Fran," said Trent. He looked around. "We can revisit this issue again later. If at that point you all still feel we're having too many meetings, we'll find a solution."

Oscar nodded.

Trent walked over to the white board. "We need to rank the twelve-month goals. Under the growth vision, the sales goal should rank a 10 and the client retention goal an 8."

"Client retention should be as important as sales," jumped in Fran. "It costs us a lot more to acquire new clients."

"I agree with Fran," said Hector.

Trent stopped to contemplate. "Client retention has certainly been our biggest problem, but sales effectiveness to me is a more important goal because client retention has a physical limit. We can only go as high as a 100%, and I'm not sure 100% is ever attainable."

"Client retention indicates if the client-centric philosophy is succeeding," said Hector. "If becoming fully client-centric is the highest ranked vision component, then client-retention should be the highest ranked goal."

"You're right," conceded Trent. "Client retention is now a 10. How should we rank the sales goal?"

"An 8 or a 9," said Hector.

"It should also be a 10," resisted Trent. "Increasing sales effectiveness can't be less important. To generate growth, we must improve our upper-tier sales effectiveness. I'd argue for it to be more important, but I'll agree to make both goals equally important."

"I'll accept that," said Fran. "The strategies for those two goals will have a big impact on our success or failure. We better design them well."

Trent's Notes

Cohegic Method Takeaways

1. Many companies develop goals in a vacuum and do not make the effort to link them back to the vision. Goals must flow from and connect to the vision — cohegic flow.

2. The choice of goals reveals to the organization how management expects to realize the vision. It is the high-level path/strategy to achieve the vision. Goals must also be in-sync with the spirit — cohegic flow.

3. Goals compete for mind share and resources. Different management members may have their favorite goals, and consciously or subconsciously, they might push the organization to focus on those goals. The management team as a whole must rank goals to clarify the thrust and avoid hidden difference of opinions.

Management and Leadership Takeaways

1. The goal identification meeting should focus on identifying goals, and not on discussing the strategies for implementing the goals. That will ensure the meeting is effective and the team spends enough time identifying the right goals.

2. Introducing change in an organization is difficult because the natural tendency is to resist change. Therefore, agents of change management must implement change quickly and simply.

Hintec's Overall Goal Hierarchy

Three-Year Vision

Client-Centric Vision (10)
Become fully client-centric: Build client-centric capabilities and deliver successfully

Growth Vision (8)
Be significantly larger in revenues, # of clients, engagement size

Recognition Vision (7)
Be considered as a premier upper-tier BI provider

Process Goal (10)
Create standard client-centric delivery processes to ensure consistent high-quality delivery

Sales Goal (10)
Improve upper-tier sales effectiveness

Success-Stories Goal (10)
Generate significant upper-tier client success stories

Resources Goal (10)
Develop consulting resources to deliver client-centric BI services

Retention Goal (10)
Improve upper-tier client retention

Advocacy Goal (8)
Advocate and publicize client success stories

Industry Goal (7)
Develop industry specific competencies

Product Goal (7)
Add functional product features to ease BI adoption

The (number) indicates relative importance among siblings.

Chapter 11: Strategies

Trent showed Watson the goals. Watson glanced over them.

"I was expecting you might grill me," said Trent.

"Not really. I want to show you the method, and then let you and your team drive its implementation. You'll make mistakes but you'll correct them. Now that you have your vision and goals in place, you must figure out how to achieve the goals. Strategy, the third component of direction, is the roadmap to your goals."

"Strategy is the big one."

Watson glanced at the lake for a moment. "You'll see two types of phenomenon. At one end of the spectrum, companies lack a visible strategy. They develop goals aplenty, but don't define the roadmap. So, it's not clear to the organization what actions it must take. Strategy becomes the best-kept secret, hidden in the mind of the CEO."

"I'm guilty of that," confessed Trent.

"On the other end, some companies treat strategies as the be-all and end-all, like an artist in love with his paintbrushes. Strategies must not exist in isolation."

Trent surmised, "Every goal must have a strategy and every strategy must be tied to a goal."

"Great summary," said Watson enthusiastically.

Trent reflected, "I think we all get consumed by the day-to-day stuff, and strategy takes a back seat."

"When your day-to-day actions don't link to your strategy and it stops evolving, you lose ground and reduce your ability to produce superior results."

"Execute and evolve strategy at the same time," commented Trent.

"Yes, update your strategies regularly otherwise they won't be worth much. You must explain to the employees how the strategies are working, or not, and what they must do differently. Everyone in Hintec must adjust their thinking and actions to match the evolving strategies."

"I suspect if the strategy evolves too fast, we may risk losing our strategic coherence."

"Agreed," said Watson. "There is another way to lose strategic coherence. If you don't detail your strategies, your employees will interpret the strategy in many different ways."

Trent nodded. "What do you think about SWOT analysis: identifying the strengths, weaknesses, opportunities, and threats?"

"Some of the ideas identified through SWOT analysis may fit in the philosophy and vision categories and others in the goals and strategy categories."

"So, you recommend SWOT analysis?"

"Yes, and other strategy models, tools and formulation methods at your disposal. Remember the tools and techniques aren't as important as the ideas you identify. It's more important to develop a coherent set of ideas and articulate them clearly."

In the next meeting, Trent looked at the employees and said, "I'll do something different today and invite my team members to explain a component each of what we've developed so far."

All the team members including Hector, VP customer service, and Simon, VP sales, went through the exercise with conviction. After they finished, Trent said, "Today, we develop the strategies for our highest ranked goals. What should be our strategy to fulfill the process goal: develop standard client-centric delivery processes?"

"Keep the process simple," pitched in Hector. "Otherwise, it'll fail."

"Good point," said Trent, as he wrote it down.

"Ensure all the departments have a role in making the delivery process successful," said the VP of HR.

"I really like that," said Trent, looking at Oscar.

"And, we should make sure the end result is that the client acknowledges the value created," said CFO Fran.

"Excellent. The three ideas we've identified are: keep the delivery process simple, ensure all teams play a role in the process, and ensure clients acknowledge the value created."

"That doesn't seem like much of a strategy," said Hector. "Calling those three ideas a strategy is an indulgence."

Trent answered calmly, "You're right, Hector. The three ideas we've identified are commonplace; nothing earth-shattering to be designated as a lofty, brilliant strategy."

Hector looked perplexed. "You're agreeing with me?"

"Yes, but consider the goal we're building a strategy for. It's an operational goal. It doesn't require a lofty strategy, but down-to-earth ideas, the type you like."

"I kinda see your point," said Hector.

"Our high-level strategy was decided when we chose the philosophies of client-centric and focus on the upper-tier."

"That's exactly right," said Fran.

"Let me clarify," said Trent. "For a goal like the sales goal, we're likely to develop an interesting and creative strategy."

"I get it," said Hector.

Trent looked at the sheet with the goals. "Let's discuss the industry goal. For which industries should we develop specific competencies?"

"Based on the customers we have now, I would say, Oil & Gas, Chemicals, Manufacturing and Healthcare," said Fran.

There were several nods. The team discussed the rest of the goals.

Later that day as Trent was answering emails, Simon walked in. Trent looked up and invited him to sit down.

"I have disturbing news," said Simon.

"What's wrong?"

"I'm getting reports Maxell's been bad-mouthing Hintec."

"In what way?"

"Spreading rumors our product doesn't deliver what we promise and is overly complex."

Trent pushed his chair back. "It's a pity he's engaging in such tactics. When we gave him the severance package, he signed the agreement not to disparage Hintec." Trent closed his eyes briefly. "What do you recommend?"

"We should contact all our clients and prospects and tell them Maxell's no longer with Hintec. Discredit him."

Trent squinted. "That's the instinctive reaction but mudslinging can become a big distraction. There must be a better way to neutralize him. I need to sleep on this."

"You seem lost in thought," asked Lori as they ate dinner.

"Maxell's back in the picture. He's bad mouthing Hintec."

"What're you going to do about it? Ask Watson?"

"No. I don't want to run to Watson every time I have a problem. In any case, Watson and I have more important things to focus on."

When Trent saw Watson that evening, he said, "This method is worthwhile. My team has asked questions reflecting deep-rooted concerns. Without going step-by-step, those questions wouldn't have come up."

"You're perceptive," said Watson. "Those questions would remain buried and continue to bother them."

"Speaking of questions, I have one. Does the goal to develop industry specific competencies, fit better as a strategy than a goal?"

"Yes, industry specific focus is more a strategy-related idea than a goal. You may decide to pursue other industries or discontinue the industry-focus. Remember, goals are more permanent than strategies."

"Sounds like I might have mixed goals and strategies."

"That's all right. The transition from a goal to a strategy to a tactic isn't black and white, but a continuum. You'll have more goal-oriented concepts in the top levels, strategy ideas in the mid levels and tactical items in the bottom."

"So, it's okay if you bucket an idea in the wrong category?"

"Over time, you'll find a better place and move it. Again, we want to respect the method, but not follow it rigidly."

"Would you remind me of your definitions once more?"

"Goals describe what we want to achieve, while strategy describes how to achieve it. Strategy indicates the unique twist, the creative solution. Tactics, the next level down are the to-do lists. At the tactical level, there's little creativity, just a decomposition of the strategy into granular action steps."

Trent mulled for a few moments. "I like our approach. We have a generic product, and on top of it we're overlaying industry specific services. It gives us great flexibility."

At the next meeting, Trent started, "Simon, what should be our strategy to improve upper-tier sales effectiveness?"

"Re-train our salespeople," replied Simon.

"We may need to replace them," sighed Trent. "We now have to sell to upper management and not IT management, and instead of leading with the product, we must lead with the client's business imperatives."

"Maybe we can use our existing salespeople," said Fran.

Trent looked at her.

"By coupling our new delivery resources, that have experience dealing with executives, with our salespeople," said Fran explaining her suggestion.

"I like that," said Trent. "Many companies do that. We could dedicate some delivery resources to the sales effort."

"We need to rebrand as client-centric," said Simon, beginning to go with the flow.

"Absolutely!" said Trent, happy to see Simon's involvement. "It'll increase sales effectiveness."

"Rebranding has a bigger role than just increasing sales effectiveness," said Hector. "Rebranding contributes directly to the growth vision. We should add it as a goal."

Looking at Hector, Trent said, "I'm happy to see you championing growth. I'll add rebranding to the goal hierarchy."

"I don't want to rain on the parade," interjected Fran. "How're we going to pay for all of this? Is the board going to sign off on all the new resources and marketing campaign?"

"Great question," said Trent. "We'll divide our effort into pieces so we can demonstrate quick and robust progress."

"I see a huge shift in the talent and resources needed to make this change happen," said Hector. "But I buy-into it. It can be a powerful way for Hintec to conquer the marketplace."

"Thanks, Hector," said Trent. "It'll be worth finding out if our approach to serve clients in a larger context succeeds."

"No kidding," said Hector.

"Venkat and Simon, would you create off-line the product strategy and present it to us," asked Trent. They agreed and Trent wrapped up the meeting. "I've created a draft strategy for the client-retention goal and I'll email it to you. Please review it and give me your ideas."

After the meeting, Trent went to see Hector.

"Hi, come in. It was a good meeting," said Hector.

"It sure was. I like how we're progressing."

"How can I help you," asked Hector as Trent sat down.

"Maxell is bad-mouthing Hintec."

"I'm disappointed to hear that," said Hector shaking his head. "I thought I knew Maxell."

"We've got to stop him. I'm looking for a simple solution. I don't want to go to our lawyers."

"I can't help you, but Barry might be able to. After all he hired Maxell at Hintec and knew him from before."

Trent cringed. He didn't want to ask his predecessor for help.

"Don't worry. Barry will be happy to help you. Call him."

"Thanks," said Trent. He went back to his office and asked Amy to set up a lunch with Barry.

That evening Trent shared with Watson, "I feel the time is right for the team to develop the strategies further down. It'll allow them to put their stamp on the strategy, and in the process develop a sense of ownership of the strategy."

"I agree with that," approved Watson.

"I have a doubt. When I looked at the strategies, they seem simple. We've created strategy out of thin air... I mean, companies go through rigorous exercises, analyze mountains of data, and use several tools. My point is should we go through a rigorous exercise to formulate strategy?"

"If you have a need?"

"Do we?" asked Trent looking at Watson.

"To penetrate a new market or introduce a new product, you might need a lot of upfront analysis and research."

"No, we're staying in the same market with the same product. You know that...."

"I'm wary of a big strategy exercise. You get a binder at the end, which only ends up adorning your bookcase. If you go through such an exercise, be sure to capture the high-points so you can communicate the strategy succinctly."

Trent pondered.

"You have a significant understanding of your marketplace and customers, and sufficient knowledge to implement the ideas," continued Watson.

"Yes, we do," agreed Trent.

"Instead of spending time to analyze now, analyze the results you see in the marketplace as a result of your initiatives. Are you able to generate demonstrable successes?"

"So you're saying base our strategy on execution results rather than on upfront analysis and postulations."

"Yes. For a major oil company deciding the course for the next fifty years, enormous research and analysis is important. Hintec on the other hand, must use a dynamic and opportunistic strategy closely coupled with its execution."

That night, as he lay on the bed, Trent said to Lori, "I have tremendous faith in Watson, and yet I wonder... there's this uneasy feeling, something bugs me."

"Well, you can be sure only when you see the results."

"That's it." He sat up. "I've been following the method religiously and as fast as I can, but we've not begun to implement anything. The board will want to see tangible progress. That's what's bothering me."

The next day the VP of engineering came to visit Trent.

"What's up," asked Trent.

"I've been thinking about the strategy for the product goal. Barry and I had decided to build the next generation of our product. I now feel we may have introduced a lot of complexity, which may have contributed in part to decreasing our client retention rate," confessed Venkat.

Trent listened with rapt attention.

"I should've known better," said Venkat, chastising himself. "My computer science professor used to say, you're not done when you can't think of features to add. Your software product is complete when you can't think of features to remove. Going forward, my strategy for the product is to create a useable, useful, and simple product."

"How difficult would it be to do that?" enquired Trent, liking what he had heard.

"The challenge is in untangling all the features we implemented on top of the modules, which have made the whole product and especially the user interface complex. Your clear choice of philosophies and direction will help my team and I figure out exactly what needs to be done."

Trent smiled and closed his eyes for a moment. "Thank you, Venkat. Thank you. I pray the board members appreciate what you, the other management members, and I have done to rewire our thinking and reinvent Hintec."

That evening, Trent asked Watson, "When can we start implementing stuff?"

"You could jump into implementation, but I'd wait until we discuss work processes and organizational design. Once we discuss execution, all the pieces will be in place."

Trent sighed.

"Okay. What would you like to start implementing?"

"Putting in place the process to hire delivery resources."

"If anything, you should explain your client-centric approach to clients and see if they'll want to pay for it."

"For them to sign-up, they'll want to see how it will help them specifically. We need marketing collaterals to explain the benefits of using our BI delivery resources. So it's rebranding that needs to be worked on first."

"This is exactly the deliberation you'll have to go through when you chart out your immediate-term objectives with your team. If you jump to execution prematurely, you'll create confusion and take your eye off the important pieces that still need to be addressed."

"Okay, I'll be patient," said Trent. He opened his portfolio and said, "I have the strategies we developed."

Looking at the sales goal's strategy, Watson said, "Your sales effectiveness strategy needs more work. It might serve you to think about what I call top sales drivers. But before we discuss them, help me understand your competition."

"Our biggest competitor is status quo. We find 75% of our prospects have never used BI software. Convincing them to use the software is the most difficult aspect."

"How do you fare against the competition?"

"Product wise no one has a big, distinct advantage. Every competitor is in the race to be current with the rest. In fact, prospects sometimes complain to us that making a decision about which product to use is difficult for them."

"What's your sales success ratio?"

"For every 12 prospects that we pursue seriously, we close one. The competition isn't eating our lunch. If we became more effective in selling and convincing the prospect to use business-intelligence, we'd do much better."

"All right, let's talk about sales drivers. They'll increase your sales effectiveness and success ratio."

"Okay," said Trent, sitting up.

"A sales driver is a factor that creates a compelling case for the purchase and/or overcomes a strong hurdle. It influences critical aspects such as the probability of closing the deal, sales cycle-time, deal profit margin, and the post-sale risk of failure."

"I can think of a large number of sales drivers."

"I bet you can, but the challenge is in identifying the top one to five. While the commonplace sales drivers are necessary, they're not sufficient. Only the top drivers have the power to take the deal to closure."

"I'd love to hear some examples."

"Sure, I'll discuss three. The first one is a compelling business event. If your prospect doesn't face a compelling business event that demands some strong action, the likelihood of closing the deal is low regardless of your product features and your salesperson's selling skills. Identifying and addressing the compelling business event will significantly increase your success ratio."

"We try to find out what's happening with the prospect, but I don't think we actively identify a compelling event. It'll be worth our while to do so."

"The second example is developing an executive-level internal champion. Because your solutions involve major change, your deals will succeed more if your salespeople are able to cultivate an executive-level champion in the client organization who can push the deal internally."

Trent was excited. "I like that idea."

Watson continued, "The third example is to mitigate or manage risk. Change creates risk. It may take time and a lot of work for the client to realize value from your solution, while the risk introduced is immediate. Therefore, the prospect's instinct is to maintain status quo. Mitigating and managing the risk introduced by your solution could be a significant sales driver."

"That's really interesting. I wonder how many deals we've lost because we ignored the technical, political or performance risks we were introducing. I like the three top sales drivers you mentioned. They apply to us. I'll add them to our sales effectiveness strategy."

"I think you should," agreed Watson. "Next time we'll discuss operationalizing your strategy, without which your strategy will only remain a set of great ideas."

"Where the rubber meets the road," said Trent as he got up to leave.

The next day Trent had lunch scheduled with Barry.

"Thanks for joining me for lunch," said Trent, as the former CEO took his seat.

"No problem," said Barry. "How're things?"

"Things are getting better. I'm learning how to tie together all the critical aspects of running the company. Creating a cohegic Hintec, as my advisor likes to say."

"I heard," said Barry. "I'm glad you're bringing order to Hintec and forcing the team to think. Something I didn't do very well. Good job."

"Thanks," beamed Trent. Feeling encouraged, he asked, "I need your help with Maxell."

"Hector called, and explained the situation," said Barry, nodding his head to indicate he understood the situation.

Trent listened carefully.

"I'll reach out to Maxell," offered Barry. "I'll do my best to make him see it's not in his long-term interest to disparage Hintec. I can't guarantee he'll listen, but I'll try."

"Barry, thank you. I'm glad I came to you for help."

In the next meeting, Trent shared with the team the three sales drivers Watson had described: compelling business event, executive-level champion, and mitigating the risk. After he described them, he said, "I've redesigned the sales effectiveness strategy to add these three sales drivers."

"These are interesting strategic ideas," remarked Hector.

"Now, we've to see if these ideas bear fruits. When we execute, we can see what works and what doesn't," said Trent.

"And, we replace what doesn't work?" asked Oscar.

"Yes. I was confused between a goal and a strategy. A goal is something we won't easily abandon. For example improving sales effectiveness will be a goal no matter what. It'll stop being a goal once we've achieved it. But we'll have no qualms about replacing a strategy if it doesn't work. For example, we think identifying a compelling business event will help us close deals. But if it doesn't, we'll replace it."

"I like it," said Hector. "It's come together."

Trent smiled and the others nodded.

Hector and Venkat came to see Trent. Hector began, "We studied the client retention strategy you put out, and realized we can implement one of the ideas right away."

"Which one?" asked Trent excitedly.

"Proactively intercepting issues before they become big."

Venkat joined in, "We'd like to approach our one hundred biggest clients and ask them what issues they're facing right now. We'll offer to have our engineers evaluate their systems to make sure things are okay."

"We won't charge them anything," explained Hector, "but I'm sure the time we spend, we'll more than make up by mitigating issues in the future. What do you think?"

"I love it!" said Trent. "This begins to fulfill our client-centric promise. I've been concerned we aren't implementing anything yet. This is a perfect item; it doesn't affect anything else. I'm curious to see how it'll impact our client turnover."

Trent's Notes

Hintec's Sales Effectiveness Strategy Hierarchy

Sales Goal (10)

Improve upper-tier sales effectiveness

Needs Strategy (10)

Improve how we develop/identify the client's need and pain

Sales Effort Strategy (10)

Improve who is part of the sales team/effort

Credibility Strategy (8)

Improve how we and our solution are perceived by prospects

Client Imperatives Strategy (10)

Change the sales approach – Lead with client business imperatives instead of leading with the product

Champion Strategy (10)

Identify an executive champion in the client organization who can sell the deal internally

Risk Strategy (10)

Mitigate/ manage risk associated with introducing our solution

Compelling Event Strategy (10)

Identify compelling business events that drive prospects to close the deal

Tag-team Strategy (9)

Create tag-teams of sales people and senior client-centric delivery resources

Industry Experts Strategy (8)

Hire renowned business experts from targeted industry sectors to enhance our credibility and relationships

The (number) indicates Relative Importance among siblings.

Trent's Notes

Cohegic Method Takeaways

1. In business literature, there are many different meanings assigned to strategies. The Cohegic method defines strategies as the "how," the unique twist in which the organization expects to achieve each of its goals. Strategies reflect the creative energy of the organization.

2. In the Cohegic method, goals are more permanent than strategies. An organization will rarely give up on a goal, but it will readily drop a strategy if it does not work. The reason being, strategies are only a hypothesis to achieve the goals.

3. Every goal must have a strategy and every strategy must be associated with a goal, to ensure cohegic flow.

Management Takeaways

1. In many organizations, strategy is the best-kept secret, hidden in the mind of the leader. As a result, the organization does not understand the actions it must take to achieve the goals. Having a well-articulated and succinct strategy is a necessity.

2. Some organizations consider strategy to be the be-all and end-all. They fall in love with their strategies and fail to recognize the signs that might indicate a strategy is not working. Strategies are only the means to an end.

3. Management must regularly evolve and update strategies to reflect what is working and what is not. A stale strategy will jeopardize the organization's performance.

Section 5: Engine

Chapters in the Engine section:

Chapter 12: Work Processes

Chapter 13: Organization Design

Chapter 14: Culture

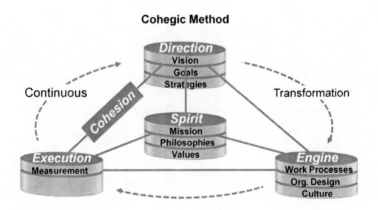

Chapter 12: Work Processes

The next evening, as Watson and Trent came out on the deck, Trent said, "The water is so calm." Then he leaned forward, pointing, "Oh, look ducks. They're paddling our way." The men watched the ducks until they paddled past them.

When they sat down, Watson started, "So far, you've laid the foundation by articulating Hintec's spirit, and you've designed the direction. Now you have to focus on crystallizing the substratum, the infrastructure, you need to execute effectively and efficiently. I'm talking about engine, the third facet in the Cohegic method."

"Do you think we'll be done with the first cycle through all the five facets before the board meeting in the second week of October?" asked Trent breaking the line of thought.

"That gives us just under six weeks. You'll need to stay focused and committed. Spirit and direction are the most time consuming facets. Engine will take time as well, but execution and cohesion will go faster because they're more about action than discussion," said Watson addressing Trent's concern.

"Okay," said Trent. "No distractions and no time to waste."

Returning to the topic at hand, Watson said, "For the engine to perform well, you must tune its three components, work processes, organization design, and culture."

"Would you include capabilities under engine?"

"Yes, good point. All your efforts to train your employees, and enhance Hintec's competencies, would fit underneath the engine. You would identify work processes for such initiatives and execute them."

"Tell me more about work processes."

"Work process designs will describe how Hintec must carry out its work; the sequence of steps, interactions, and handoffs. Clear processes increase efficiency and productivity by making it easy for everyone to see what needs to happen and when. Work processes are the pillars of excellent execution."

"We need to do a better job in this area."

"Yes, you do. Successful companies are built on consistency. Well-designed and well-executed work processes are the only way to achieve consistency."

"One of our new goals is to create delivery processes to ensure consistent high-quality delivery."

Watson acknowledged with a slight nod, and continued, "Work processes are living, evolving artifacts. Respect work processes, but at the same time, don't follow them so rigidly that you become bureaucratic."

"I recognize that. I'm not for bureaucracy."

"I divide work processes into core and auxiliary. Core processes are directly responsible for generating and preserving revenue and have a significant impact on clients. They include processes for developing products and services, improving competencies, marketing, selling, customer service, and so on."

"And auxiliary processes?"

"They're for support, such as billing, accounting, payroll, and inventory management. Auxiliary processes are essential, but don't always distinguish the company from its competitors or create direct value for customers."

"Are auxiliary less important than core processes?"

"No, because if they don't work well the company can't function. I distinguish between the two types to help you decide what you and the management team must spend time designing and what you can delegate."

"You won't find me complaining if we delegate the design of all the processes."

Watson smiled. "I'm sure you won't. Designing work processes can be involved, but it's critical for you to make sure Hintec designs effective core processes that tie back to your goals and reflect your strategies."

"Cohegic flow," commented Trent.

"That's right," said Watson animatedly.

Simon and Trent had a prospect meeting that day. When they met at the elevator bank, the VP of sales shared, "I just heard GenceSoft is discontinuing their pricing discount."

"Really?" said Trent with a big grin.

"Yes. They had a management shakeup."

"None of the other players reduced their prices, so I bet the pressure was finally too much for them," said Trent, satisfied with himself, as they entered the elevator.

"The price discount hurt them. The other players spread rumors that GenceSoft was reducing prices to compensate for serious issues with their product."

"So how much does this help us?" asked Trent.

"We had only one other prospect who was considering GenceSoft, but they had already told us they were in the market for a pure business-intelligence solution as opposed to the gamut of modules GenceSoft was offering."

"This is good news. Maybe now NAPIT Oil will give us a second consideration. See if we can get an appointment."

"Okay, I'll get on it," said Simon.

"We've crystallized who we are and where we're headed," started Trent in the next meeting. "Now, we've to figure out the vehicle to get us there. Work processes are the mechanics of our organization's engine. If you are building a sports car you would pick different parts than if you are building a minivan."

"If we keep our spirit in mind," said the VP of customer service, "our most important process is to help clients make superior decisions. That encapsulates visiting with clients, understanding needs, solving data issues, using our product to do the analysis, and providing meaningful insights clients can use to make critical decisions."

"That's an excellent summary, Hector," said Trent enthusiastically.

Oscar smiled, happy to see the two get along.

"Should we look at our goals to identify the processes we need?" asked Fran.

"Great suggestion," replied Trent. He looked at the sheet with the goals and rattled off several processes, "A process to deliver high-quality client-centric services; process to develop BI delivery resources; process to develop industry-specific competencies; process to add functional features; sales process; client retention process, and a rebranding process."

"Will we become bureaucratic?" asked the CFO.

"Only if we become a slave to the processes, but we're not doing that. By defining the processes, we increase clarity. When something fails, we'll know which process it's a part of and then we'll be able to fix that process," said Trent.

"Okay," said Fran.

"Let's start with the process, delivering high-quality client-centric services," said Trent. He got up and walked to the white board. "Let me list some of the steps I see for this process."

After he finished writing the steps, Fran asked, "Where's our strategy reflected in the design of this work process?"

"Great question," said Trent emphatically. "Let me look at the strategy for the delivery process goal."

After going through the strategy sheet, Trent said, "We had identified three strategy ideas. Looking at them, first, we need a process-step to gain the client's recognition of the value we create. Second, our process so far is simple so we're adhering to that strategy idea. The third strategy idea was every department must play a role in the success of this supercritical process."

"That's a tricky one because all the steps in this process will be conducted by the delivery resources," said Hector.

"This is such an important process, surely the rest of us can contribute to it," implored Trent.

"How? By hanging around the client site and watching over the shoulders of our delivery resources?" questioned Hector.

"No, the rest of us aren't going to be present physically at the client site. Yet, all of us have a big role to play," said Trent searching for an answer.

"How?" pushed Hector again.

Everyone pondered. Then Trent said, "This process will be successful only when we set the right expectations when we sell, and answer the questions: How will the process work? How does it create value? Once clients understand, they'll be prepared for the changes. They'll know how to recognize and acknowledge the value we create. Let me clarify. This isn't about setting high expectations, just setting the right expectations, and educating the clients."

"All right," accepted Hector.

"Also," continued Trent, "our delivery resources will rely on the rest of us. They'll need support to solve issues, answer product-related questions, and leverage our management team to help in tricky client situations. The rest of us play a critical role behind the scenes. We're the backbone; our delivery resources are the face. In purely consulting companies, the consultants are responsible for the entire delivery. In our case, the delivery resources create value standing on the shoulders of our product. We need close interaction between our external, customer-facing resources and our internal resources."

"Excellent," said the VP of HR. "I like the way you've described the interaction between the groups, making it a tight-knit, well-orchestrated effort."

"Thanks, Oscar. This point's important for one more reason. The rest of us must familiarize ourselves with the client's business imperatives. When an issue comes up, the first thing we should do is review the needs of the customer. Doing so will tune all of us toward being client-centric."

"We need an internal IT system to capture this information so everyone can have quick access to it," said Venkat.

"You're right, we've overlooked the IT aspect. Would you create a task for your IT staff to create a system that can help us with our client-centric services?"

"Sure," said Venkat.

"I had read about operationalizing strategy," said Oscar. "Today, we've actually accomplished the link between strategy and operations."

Trent smiled. "Let's stop here for today. Why don't we develop the draft processes associated with the other goals off-line and then present it to the group. I can develop the draft for the sales process."

"I can do the draft rebranding process," offered Simon.

Trent nodded. Looking at Hector, he asked, "Would you like to develop the draft for the client retention process?"

Hector nodded.

Oscar offered to develop the draft for the recruiting process, Venkat the process to add functional features, and Fran, the process to develop industry specific competencies.

As everyone walked out, Trent asked Oscar to stay back.

"We've included employees in our meetings," said Trent. "They've contributed, but for the most part they've been observers. I'm happy to continue to invite them if they find it valuable. Would you get a pulse check from the employees?"

"Actually, I have," said the VP of HR. "I've been getting feedback. I was in the process of compiling it all to share it with you and the group. The employees appreciate the transparency and the opportunity to see first-hand the deliberations and discussions. Other employees have expressed an interest in attending as well. The timing is right for your series of town-hall meetings; it'll allow more employees to hear from you."

"Speaking about which, at each town-hall meeting I shall ask at least one other management team member to join me and have them do half the presentation."

"That's a great idea. I loved it when in one meeting you asked each of us to describe a component to the employees."

"Thanks for that feedback. I'll do that in all the meetings going forward." Then he sighed. "Designing work processes is a lot of work."

"It's overwhelming because we haven't done it on a regular basis," said Oscar. "If you don't clean your house for fifteen years, it'll be back-breaking when you finally do it."

"You're right. We have to bite the bullet and go through it. The subsequent cycles through the facets will hopefully be easier."

"Oh...," said Oscar. "I wanted to tell you, I discussed the strategy for attracting BI delivery resources, with my team. We've come up with a combination of ideas ranging from internet job boards to employee referral bonuses. I'll summarize all the ideas and e-mail them to you. If you like the approach, give us the green light, and we'll get moving."

"As much as I'd like to give you approval, I've to wait until the board meeting to make sure the board is with me on this new direction. In the meantime, why don't you ask your team to get a head start by doing some of the legwork?"

"I will. Do you have a sense for how many BI delivery resources we'll need?"

"That's a good question. I'll guess... it'll take about one third of a full-time equivalent for each upper-tier client. Since our goal is 200 to 300 such clients, I suspect eighty to a hundred resources when we're fully staffed."

That evening Trent showed Watson the list of processes and asked, "When you talked about identifying work processes, you talked about looking at the overall business. In our meeting today, we instead identified processes that were inspired by our goals. Which approach is correct?"

"You're perceptive," said Watson. "Your goals will typically pertain only to things you need to do better or different. There's much more to Hintec than these goals; it has operational aspects. Work processes are about all aspects, not just the strategic aspects. The timeframe for work processes is also much larger. For example, you have a vision to become client-centric and an associated work process to deliver client-centric services. Once you achieve the vision, it'll go away, but the work process will be around forever."

"I see what you're saying. Did we make a mistake?"

"No, not really. As I've said before, this is about cycling through the facets. With subsequent cycles through the design of work processes, you'll cover more breadth and depth. To begin with, it's okay to focus only on the work processes related to the strategic goals and not operational imperatives."

"Okay. Do we have to create a work process for every goal?"

"Not immediately because it'll be difficult to take on so much all at once. Focus on the important ones and delegate the rest or work on them later. When we discuss execution, we'll develop a quarterly plan listing your immediate priorities. The quarterly plan will also help you decide which work process designs you need immediately."

"We also figured out today that work processes and strategy are parallel concepts."

"Very good," said Watson with a satisfied look. "Both work processes and strategy are about fulfilling the goal. Work process design must reflect the strategy, and, hence, you must design work processes after you have crystallized the strategy. Strategy discussions are about creative thinking;

work process discussions are about the systematic arrangement of the sequence of steps."

"I promised the team I'll develop the draft sales process. I'm sure I'll get it done much faster if you help me."

"Sure, I'd be happy to. When we meet tomorrow evening, let's take up the sales process."

As he was about to leave his office at the end of the next day, Trent's phone rang. He answered it. It was the former CEO.

"Hi Trent," said Barry. "I met with Maxell, today."

"And...," asked Trent anxiously.

"He agreed to stop bad-mouthing Hintec."

"Great news," said Trent.

"I was quite emphatic. I think he got the message. But keep your eyes and ears open. Let me know if you find he hasn't stopped and then we can think of other remedies."

"Thanks, Barry. Thanks a bunch. I hope Maxell doesn't trouble us any more."

When Trent went to see Watson after dinner, Watson began, "You ready to design the sales process?"

"Yeah, sure."

"Do you have a sales process now?"

"We have an informal sales process at best."

"Does every salesperson follow their own method?"

"Pretty much."

"In many companies," said Watson, "there's no formal sales process. Companies measure salespeople by how many deals they close and overlook whether they follow a consistent, efficient process."

"Well, if a salesperson's closing deals, you should be happy," countered Trent. "Good salespeople are extremely difficult to come by. Leave them alone to do their thing."

Watson smiled, "Okay, then let's not develop the sales process. Let's keep things the way they are."

Trent thought about it with a bemused look on his face.

"Well, we've got to develop a sales process because…."

"Because, why?"

"We want the salespeople to be more effective at selling to upper-tier clients. They're not used to doing that. We need to figure out the steps so it becomes easier for them."

"Your issue is you have a new upper-tier strategy, and if you don't manage the sales process you won't be able to execute your strategy. Without a sales process, you'll have no visibility and transparency into what the salespeople are doing. Are their sales messages consistent? Which sales drivers are succeeding? If your salespeople act as lone rangers, you'll have no collective intelligence on customers and the marketplace."

"We do have deal meetings to review the deals."

"Do you follow the same level of rigor that you recommend your clients follow with their business-intelligence?"

Trent became quiet. Watson waited.

"No. We haven't used our BI tool to look at our sales-related intelligence," confessed Trent. "I guess because we've not had a consistent well-defined sales process, we've not systematically looked at our sales drivers."

Watson smiled. "I don't want to be harsh, but Hintec isn't using its own tools. If I were your client, that'd be disconcerting to me."

Trent clamped his jaw and lowered his eyes. "I see the benefit to sales management," he said. "But I can see why salespeople don't want to be constrained. Selling's about being creative and flexible. You can't be tied to a fixed script."

"A sales process isn't a script, and it isn't about rigidity," replied Watson. "It's about providing a framework, within which a salesperson has the flexibility to respond to the prospect and the situation."

Trent looked doubtful. Watson continued, "A sales process does add administrative burden. Hence, it's important to design the sales process and related artifacts such that you ask salespeople to record only critical information."

"At a minimum."

"Next, assign administrative resources to help salespeople capture the data."

"I like that."

Watson continued, "At every stage of the sales process, the focus of the salesperson should be to gain information. Is the prospect desirable? Is it the right type of customer for Hintec? Is the account win-able? Is there a current opportunity, an important and urgent need that'll allow Hintec to sell the prospect its product and services in the near future?"

Trent waved his hand dismissing Watson's point. "They understand all of that, they're doing it."

"Are you willing to guarantee it?" challenged Watson. "Without a clearly followed sales process, you can't guarantee your salespeople are collecting this information or consistently making good decisions."

Trent paused and deliberated. "Watson, I realized something... when you described designing work processes and the need to do it, I agreed with you. However, when I thought about the practicalities, I realized such a formal process would be very difficult to sell to the troops. Forget the troops. Even I'm struggling to buy it. Not because it's a bad idea but because I don't feel it's realistic to expect it'll become part of how we sell. I can see my conflict. I agree with you conceptually, but disagree practically."

"Well, we've hit the crux of the matter. Organizations and human beings know what's right, but they don't do it because it's difficult to do. An overweight person knows that he or she should avoid desserts full of fat, yet yields to the temptation."

"So what do we do?"

"It's a question of leadership. Do you have the fortitude to go through and standardize your sales effort? You were happy to force the others to follow a process, but are backing off when it comes to sales. Without a systematic sales effort, Hintec's sales performance will be a slave to its star salespeople. They'll choose to behave in the manner they like and it will undermine Hintec's culture and your initiatives."

"We don't want that."

Watson became quiet, giving Trent time to think.

"I'm sorry. You're right," conceded Trent. "I can't judge initiatives based solely on how hard they'll be to implement. We have to change the culture. Unless I know what the salespeople are doing, and what their approach is, I can't tell if we'll be successful with our upper-tier thrust. Simon will hate it but we have no choice."

"Very good," said Watson. "Let's design the process."

After they designed and drew up the process, Trent said, "Following this sales process will help us become a sophisticated sales engine. I can see now, without it we wouldn't have a dream of making our salespeople stick with our strategic ideas."

"I hate to say it, but you still have no dream of this happening unless you implement the tenets of good execution — measure, monitor, and follow-through."

The next morning Trent went to see Simon. He reviewed the sales process and the steps the salespeople need to follow.

Simon frowned. "Salespeople want to sell. They don't want to write reports that no one's going to look at. They're going to enter garbage in the system and that's what will come out in the reports, a huge waste of time."

Trent pointed his finger at Simon. "That's your job, making sure salespeople don't enter garbage. You'll have to monitor what our salespeople are doing and how they're doing it."

"They're not rookies," Simon pushed back. "These are experienced people, and they don't like anyone looking over their shoulders. If they don't deliver, we'll fire them."

"Yes, and it'll take nine months before you figure that out. Then you'll replace them and hope the next person works out."

"Well, I can't sit here watching over these guys. I'll drive myself crazy. Like you, I'm a great salesperson, and I like to hunt. That's what gets me out of bed every morning."

"That's exactly right, Simon, that's exactly right."

"What do you mean?"

"You're a great salesperson. The question is why you are in the role of VP of sales."

"I'm not sure what you're saying," said Simon with a pensive look. "I'm a good leader and I can motivate the troops. I kept the team together in spite of all the things that happened in the last few months."

Trent didn't want to get into an argument, so he wrapped up the discussion and excused himself.

At the management meeting, Trent started, "Before we start today, I want to ask you what you've heard about this method."

One of the employees said, "This is unique. I haven't experienced being in high-level meetings at other companies. It's nice to watch all of you in action and learn how you think."

Another employee added, "We want to learn about the strategy. We want to know there's a well thought out plan."

"I'm glad to hear that," said Trent looking at Simon. He turned back to the employees and said, "If you have feedback you weren't comfortable sharing here, please send it to Oscar so he can bring it to our attention anonymously."

Looking at the team, Trent said, "Today, our objective is to finish the design of the work processes. We designed our delivery process in the last meeting. Watson and I have developed our sales process." He passed out copies.

"Here is the client-retention process," said Hector, handing out his copies.

Simon, Venkat, Fran and Oscar passed out copies of the processes they had developed. As they reviewed the designs, Hector said, "Our processes are not as concise as yours."

"Well, I had help from Watson," said Trent.

The team refined and approved the work process designs.

Later in the day, Trent stopped by Venkat's office. Venkat wasn't in. Trent turned around to walk away when Venkat called him from behind. "Trent, were you looking for me?"

"Yes, I was."

Venkat entered his office and invited Trent in. Trent sat down and said, "Watson asked me a question, that's been bothering me."

"What did he ask?"

"Why we weren't using our own business-intelligence tools? He asked that in the context of our sales effort but it got me thinking. Can we use our tool to analyze our customer service data?"

"I'll assign an engineer, but I don't want to raise your hopes. In order to extract meaningful intelligence we should have been collecting the right raw data. What are you looking for?"

"A better understanding of the patterns of our service calls. I realize we might not find anything, but it's clear to me we need to use our own tool in as many aspects of our business as it makes sense. If nothing else, this exercise may tell us what data the customer service team should begin collecting to extract meaningful intelligence in the future."

"I see your point," said Venkat. "Let me think. The customer service department has all the raw data from the service calls. I'll see if we can set up some data cubes so we can correlate the data in multiple ways, slice and dice it, see if there are any patterns."

"That'll be great. Let's see what we can find."

Trent's Notes

Upper-Tier Sales Process

Generate upper-tier leads

Is lead worth pursuing? — No

(Does lead fit our upper-tier profile?) — Lead Generation Stage

Yes (Lead is now considered a prospect)

Incisively qualify the prospect (research them in depth, visit with them)

Is prospect desire-able? — No

Yes

(Should we commit time to develop needs, solution & proposal?) — Prospect Qualification Stage

Understand prospect's business imperatives (involve Hintec delivery experts), pain and needs, to find an opportunity. Identify a compelling event, and an executive champion.

Is opportunity win-able? — No

Yes

(Can we address prospect needs? Does our solution have an edge?) — Opportunity Development Stage

Collaborate with prospect to develop solution & engagement plan. Set right expectations. Mitigate solution risk.

Solution Development Stage

Understand what prospect expects in proposal. Present a winning proposal.

Proposal Stage

Deal closed? — No

Yes

Deal Closure Stage

Continue to delivery processes

Trent's Notes

Cohegic Method Takeaways

1. Work process designs describe how an organization carries out its work; the necessary sequence of steps, interactions, and handoffs.

2. The design of work processes must incorporate the strategy, thus operationalizing the strategy — cohegic flow. Without well-designed and well-monitored work processes an organization cannot execute its strategies sufficiently and successfully.

3. Great brands are built on consistency, and without good work processes there is no consistency. Efficient and productive execution requires good work processes.

4. While work processes are important, the organization must retain its flexibility and not become bureaucratic by becoming a slave to the work processes.

Hintec's Core Work Processes

1. Client-centric delivery process
2. BI delivery resources development process
3. Industry-specific competency development process
4. Product features enhancement process
5. Sales process
6. Client retention process
7. Rebranding and advocacy process

Chapter 13: Organization Design

The next evening, as the sun hid behind a cluster of scattered clouds, the sky displayed a beautiful mix of blue and orange. The two men took their seats on the deck.

"I hope your team clearly sees how everything we've discussed links and flows," asked Watson.

"We do," answered Trent. "The link between vision, goals, and strategies was expected, but the link between strategy and work processes was an eye-opener. We're making progress toward a cohegic Hintec."

"Good," said Watson with a sense of satisfaction. "Now we have to extend that cohegic flow to the design of your teams. Organizational design, the second engine component, is our next stop."

"Is it mainly roles and responsibilities?"

"Yes. Often companies design their teams out of thin air. Executives lobby for and accumulate responsibilities as a show of strength."

"How do you prevent the horse-trading?"

"Design the organization chart based on the spirit, direction, and work processes without regard to the current management members; then decide who should be assigned to which role. This way the org chart will be based on logic and not on people considerations."

"I'm afraid of spending a whole lot of time on org design. Why can't we just look at the management team members and decide the teams? That would be expedient and place the resources we have."

"It may be expedient but it won't be the design that serves Hintec best."

"Why not?"

"The purpose of the organization design isn't to find a place to house the management team members; it's to enable the most efficient execution of the work processes. Organizational design must be based on the logic behind your goals, strategies and work processes," reiterated Watson.

"Cohegic flow," said Trent as he bobbed his head. "I was expecting org chart design would be easy. Create roles for the head of sales, marketing, engineering, customer service, HR, IT and finance, and then move on."

Watson smiled. "Patience my friend. Those customary roles are not in tune with your strategic thrust. Your org chart must serve as a constant reminder to Hintec to be in-sync with its strategic thrust. Wouldn't you want that?"

"Yes, I would."

"Okay. Why don't you and I develop a draft org chart for you to present to your team?"

Trent agreed, "We'll progress faster that way."

"Let's look at your goals and work processes."

Watson looked at the sheets with the goals and the work processes, and then said, "At the highest level, Hintec needs three teams. Two teams reflect the goal hierarchy and the third reflects the operational needs of Hintec."

"What three teams do you see?"

"A team to deliver client-centric services, a team to focus on growth and related capabilities, and a team to manage all the administrative aspects."

"Would all of Hintec fall within one of those three teams?"

"Yes. Let's discuss each team. The client-centric services team would comprise of the client-interfacing business-intelligence delivery resources you'll hire, and your existing customer service team."

Trent deliberated for a second and then said, "Let's call this the value team. They're client-centric, but their ultimate purpose specified in our strategies and work processes is to deliver value and help the clients recognize that value."

Watson smiled broadly. "Very good, I like how you tie your strategy, work process and organization design together in your explanation. Underneath the value team, you would have a delivery team for each industry sector you've chosen."

"That's good. It matches our strategy to deliver industry-specific business-intelligence services. Do we need a client retention team under the value team?"

"No. Client retention is a primary responsibility for the entire value team. Client retention and client referrals are two key metrics for tracking the value team's performance."

"Okay," said Trent.

"The next high-level team focuses on growth and capabilities. Its members must figure out how to continue generating growth by enhancing capabilities and delivery."

"Didn't my team and I just figure all that out?"

"Yes, you did. We're now designing a growth team whose job is to do it on an on-going basis and in conjunction with the other two high-level teams. The growth team would include several sub-teams: process and performance, marketing, sales, customer advocacy, engineering, strategic HR, and strategic IT."

Trent looked intrigued.

"I'll explain and justify each one of the sub-teams," said Watson. "The process and performance team would facilitate evolution of the goals and strategies, measure strategic progress and operational performance, and improve work process designs."

"Will this team ensure Hintec stays cohegic?"

"Yes. It's similar to the role I had when I worked for Globez."

Trent nodded.

Watson continued, "I've included the marketing and sales teams under the growth team, because they're the vehicles to acquire new clients and produce growth."

"What about engineering?"

"Improving your product capabilities and capabilities in general is strategic to your growth. That's why engineering is part of the growth team."

"You mentioned customer advocacy. That's an interesting term."

"Many companies have a role called product management which is typically part of their marketing team. Product managers interface with customers to determine what features they want and then work with the engineering team to develop those features."

"Our marketing team didn't have a product management function. Determining which features to build was a constant contention between engineering and sales. I was part of the problem," admitted Trent.

"Client advocacy is my name for the product management team."

"I like it," said Trent. "Now that team will know to focus on the client rather than the product."

"To round off the growth team, we have the sub-teams of strategic HR and strategic IT. Many companies treat HR and IT only as administrative aspects of the business, which gives them no seat at the strategic table. I like to split HR and IT into strategic and administrative parts and have each part report to the appropriate chain of command."

"That makes sense. In Hintec, HR plays a strategic role. That could be because Oscar's a mature executive and understands the issues. IT is shadowed a little bit, because we're a software company and IT reports into engineering. I need to decide if we should keep it that way. Speaking about which, I wonder who'll lead the growth team."

"Don't worry yet about who'll serve in these roles."

"I'm not sure I want to hire a bunch of additional management team members."

"Creating a role doesn't mean you need a new person. You can assign one person to multiple roles. We'll discuss it once we've completed the design," said Watson. "The last high-level team is the administrative team. Underneath it I'd include finance, accounting, legal, procurement, administrative HR, and IT."

"So all the auxiliary work processes are the responsibility of the administrative team," observed Trent.

Watson nodded.

"You use team and not department," commented Trent.

"I like team because it sounds collaborative, more flexible."

"Okay."

"Take care to assign the same title to all your direct reports. Either they're all senior VPs or they're all CXOs. Those three roles are equal in power and significance, the three legs of Hintec. You don't want one to dominate the others."

"I like your logic behind the design, but I have a concern. You come from a big corporation. Hintec is mid-sized. If we get too bloated, we could become inefficient."

Watson's face turned serious. "You could be right. The only way to tell if the design is valid is to recheck the logic.

Hintec has adopted new philosophies, visions, goals and strategies. It's a complete and ambitious overhaul. You need to structure the organization appropriately or you'll short-change the spirit and direction."

"Hmm...," said Trent, still struggling with the design.

"As in the design of vision, goals, and strategies, you'll find subjectivity in organizational design. There's no one right answer. A good design is easy to explain. In subsequent cycles, you'll improve the design and make it more efficient. You'll change it no matter how much you work on it now. Remember, progress and not perfection."

"You're right. I keep forgetting this is only the first cycle."

"You also need a box for the legal team. I know you use an outside law firm, but it's good to list them as well, so they feel part of Hintec. Having identified the teams, now you should be ready to assign people."

"I've been thinking about who could fill the roles, and I see several gaps."

"First, look at the qualities needed to lead a team and see who has those qualities. Then see if they have the interest. If any board or management member pressures you to make a sub-optimal choice, use the team design to explain Hintec's needs."

"This is going to be interesting."

"To bolster your argument, define clearly all the lead role responsibilities. The sales lead role needs particular attention. Hintec's sales leader's responsibilities should be to work the sales process, manage the sales pipeline, and not sell personally."

"I was afraid of that. Simon isn't the best candidate for that role but I'm afraid I'll lose him if I strip him of the title."

"Don't tell him he's not good for the job. Explain the logic behind the org design and the requirements for the role. Then ask him if he wants to do it and if he has the ability."

"I'll tell him the VP sales will no longer make commissions from personal sales, but be compensated based on overall revenue and profits. That'll get his attention," said Trent. "What do you see as the responsibilities of the CEO?"

"Ensure cohesion between spirit, direction, engine, and execution. Build a self-perpetuating and mature Hintec that makes rhythmic progress by cycling through the facets, and, thereby, overcomes threats and exploits opportunities to deliver sustained growth. If you can accomplish that, you can spend your time on the golf course."

"Cheers to that."

"Of course, it's easier said than done, but the more you're able to do it, the more time and energy you'll have to think about the next level for Hintec. If you find yourself overworked all the time, it's an indication you aren't succeeding in helping Hintec mature."

"I hear you, but what you're describing is utopian. Things will happen, and I'll be needed to make decisions."

"Sure, for major decisions and issues. But if you're involved in every little aspect, you'll be the bottleneck. Sometimes leaders are too involved because they're afraid to let go. They don't want to share credit or are not confident things will work. Such an organization cannot grow beyond the leader. Your role is to coach and mentor Hintec to deal with the issues and opportunities, not in an isolated and ad-hoc manner, but in a cohegic manner where they follow the systematic thought process and deliberate on all factors and facets."

"I liked the part about spending time on the golf course," joked Trent.

Watson smiled. "I'm not advocating you spend your time on the golf course. What I'm saying is you have to be involved at the right level. If you operate at a lower level, you'll limit yourself and your management team. Operate at too high a level, and you disconnect from the organization."

"I get it," said Trent, absorbing what Watson was saying.

"Of course, your behavior and your management style, all influence Hintec's culture, which is our next stop."

Trent shared the team design with the Chairman. Cedric endorsed the design. For the next meeting, Trent did not invite any employees. He displayed the team chart on the screen, and emphasized, "We designed the teams solely on the logic behind our goals, strategies, and work processes, and without any political or people considerations."

"Who's going to lead the three high-level teams?" asked Hector, VP customer service, jumping right to the thought foremost in everyone's mind.

"I have some ideas but I haven't decided anything yet. In any case, we must first agree on the design of the teams and the associated logic, and then think about assigning the roles. Do you agree with the logic? Is it evident?"

Oscar, VP HR, ran his hand over his bald head. When no one responded, Trent said, "Let me explain the logic."

After he finished, Fran asked, "A process and performance team?"

"We need someone to stay on top of improving our strategy, metrics, and processes; otherwise something will fall through the cracks. All the teams, from sales and delivery to engineering will be busy doing their parts. We need a team that takes input from all the teams and formulates ways to improve our work processes across teams."

"Should the sales team be part of the value team, since they're more operational, and the salespeople will have to work closely with the delivery resources?" asked Hector.

"Watson and I recognized sales as strategic to us and about growing," said Trent, "so it made sense to us to keep it part of the growth team. This design isn't meant to be perfect and we'll revisit it once we see how things work."

"I guess the question on everyone's mind is who's going to serve in these roles?" said Fran.

"And, I appreciate that, but first, let's be sure everyone agrees with the roles as laid out here. I'm happy to consider suggestions or to answer any more questions."

"The concept of the three overall teams makes sense," said Oscar. "There are a lot of sub-teams, but we're significantly reinventing Hintec."

The other team members looked thoughtful, but no one commented further, and Trent adjourned the meeting.

As they walked out, Trent caught up with Oscar. "Let's go to your office." Once they sat down, Trent asked, "What're your thoughts? Who should lead the three teams?"

Oscar looked thoughtful.

Trent continued, "Are you concerned HR won't be reporting directly to me? I mean HR and not you, because you're a candidate for one of the top three jobs."

Oscar shook his head. "I like the separation of strategic and administrative HR. HR gets the right visibility being integral to the growth team as opposed to serving it from the outside."

"What's the right role for you?" probed Trent. "Would leading one of the three teams interest you?"

"I don't have the skills to lead the growth or the value team," replied Oscar. "I could lead the administrative team and do a good job... but I'm not interested. I'm one year from retirement. I'll continue in the HR role. This would be a great opportunity for Fran and she'd do a good job."

"I appreciate that. You'll always be an important advisor to me. What is the right role for Hector?"

"The only one that might fit Hector is the value team, but I'm not sure he has the experience," said Oscar.

"I'm with you. And, I don't see Simon leading sales."

"I'm taken aback," said Oscar. "I thought you liked him."

"I do like him. He's a great salesman, but he doesn't have the sales management experience or the interest to learn it."

Trent made his next appointment with the VP of customer service. When he met with Hector, he went right to the point, "What're your thoughts on the team design?"

Hector thought about it. Trent waited anxiously.

"I think my time with Hintec has come to an end."

"Excuse me," said Trent startled. "I had no intention of offending you. We designed the chart without regard to anyone."

Hector nodded. "I know. I see the logic. This decision isn't sudden. From the day we first discussed becoming client-centric, I've realized I don't have the skill-set or the mindset for it. I've worked in product-centric companies and I like doing that. Client-centricity is right for Hintec, but it's not a fit for me."

Trent looked lost.

"I'm happy to continue leading customer service, until you find a replacement, and I'd appreciate it, if I had a role in Hintec and a paycheck until I found a new job."

"This isn't what I was expecting. I wonder what the board...."

"You don't have to worry about that. I'm not leaving because of any differences with you. Hintec is changing and you need a different set of players. I wish you and Hintec all the very best with all sincerity."

"Thanks. I appreciate the way you have presented your departure and your reason for leaving. I must say I'm surprised, and I have... more respect for you."

"Thanks for saying that. As far as finding a replacement, among my direct reports I recommend Jose Hernandez. He's progressive in his thinking and a good fit for your future thrust."

"Good suggestion. Jose is probably the most experienced among all our customer service directors."

Next, Trent went to see the VP of sales. After he sat down, he tapped Simon's desk with his fingers a few times. Simon looked on.

Trent started, "You're the best salesperson in the team, but the sales leader role is about managing the sales team full-time instead of being the top salesperson."

"What're you saying?" asked Simon nervously.

"I'm suggesting you'll create a lot more value for Hintec and yourself by focusing all your energies on selling instead of distracting yourself by managing the team."

"I want to be VP sales. I can be the best salesperson and the sales leader. I don't see the need to change."

"Simon, if you see this only from the viewpoint of having a title, then...."

"This isn't about the title. I'm the best person for the job."

Trent sighed. "I promise you'll make more money just focusing on selling."

"How?" asked Simon, his ears perking up.

"We're eliminating from the sales management role any commission from personal deals, so the leader can focus on managing the entire sales team."

"You can't do that."

"It's done. I've talked to Oscar and Cedric about that."

"You're serious?" said Simon, disturbed to hear that.

"Yes."

Simon dropped his shoulders, "I don't like it."

"Simon, the sky's the limit if you focus on selling. I'll make sure you get the respect, recognition, and reward as the best salesperson in the company. We'll be able to project you as a true star."

Simon thought about it. Then he asked, a little dejectedly, "Will I get to help decide who'll be the next VP sales?"

"Absolutely! You and I can brainstorm about that later."

"Okay," said Simon reluctantly.

"Thank you, Simon. I appreciate it."

"I appreciate your confidence in me," said Fran, when Trent offered her the job of the leader of the administrative team. "This will allow me to grow further."

"I know you'll do a great job and yes, I agree, it's a good move up for you. Hintec grows when all of us grow."

"I've started to enjoy working with you," Venkat told Trent, when Trent visited with him, "but I understand if I'm not going to report to you anymore."

"Till we find someone to lead the growth team, I'll lead it," said Trent, "so we'll still be interacting. Also, we'll all still continue to be part of the same management team."

"Dealing with people was my biggest issue," said Trent that night as he lay on the bed.

Lori sat besides reading her book.

"You're right," she agreed.

"We're reorganizing and compared to the last reorganization, this one's going smoothly. Hector offered to leave on his own accord and Simon's agreed to step down."

"Really?"

"Yes. I'm surprised it's worked so well," said Trent. He then got up and sat on the recliner to do the recliner exercise.

The next morning Venkat knocked on Trent's door. "I have some of the early results from the analysis of the customer service data. Is this a good time?"

"Yeah, sure. Come in."

"Should we call Hector?" asked Venkat as he took a seat.

"Yes, let's do that."

Trent called Hector. He was in a meeting and said he would join them in a few minutes.

"As I read the analysis, its findings are logical," said Venkat. "We should've realized it on our own."

"What does it say?" asked Trent impatiently.

"Two findings. First, we correlated the number of calls in a given month against specific product features."

"And?"

"We see a pattern. We found that a majority of the calls are around specific product features."

"Which?"

"It's not stationary."

"What do you mean?"

"I mean over time the set of features that generate the maximum calls changes."

"Then how can you say you see a pattern?"

"The pattern is that in any given quarter, the majority of the calls are around the new features introduced in the previous quarters. As we've accelerated the release of new features, our service calls have gone up. Now, I'll admit part of the reason is, we've been under pressure, and we've not had the luxury of thoroughly testing our new features."

"Sounds like quality assurance is happening not in our labs, but in the field. Clients are the ones finding the bugs."

Venkat looked sheepish. He said, "Look, Trent. I'll admit it's the bugs. But it's also the fact that as we've released these incongruent features, they've complicated our user interface, confusing our users."

"Venkat, I understand you. I now appreciate the power of unintended consequences. When I pushed for those features, I was thinking only about sales and not on what impact it creates on the product, and on customer service."

Trying to lift spirits, Venkat said, "But there is a silver lining. If we release features in a well-managed manner, our customer service calls will likely go down."

"You're right, they should. Because we're client-centric, our goal now is a reliable product, rather than be in the mad-race to one-up the competition based on features."

"A reliable, simpler, and useable software will create the most value for our clients," underscored Venkat.

Hector walked in. They invited him to take a seat and brought him up to speed on the conversation.

Looking at Venkat, Trent asked, "You said there were two findings. What was the second?"

"Yes, tell us," said Hector.

"We looked at the service calls from another dimension — the complexity of the calls. While new features caused the highest volume of calls, those calls weren't time consuming. There were another set of calls where the issue resolution consumed a long time."

"Which type of calls?" asked Hector.

"Before I tell you both that, let me share a revelation. The clients who had these types of calls typically left us in the subsequent six months."

"You're kidding me," said Trent, almost jumping out of his seat. "If you have figured that out, then we've found the secret to our success."

Venkat smiled. "I'll remind you, the finding is logical and commonsense."

"Tell us," said Trent with a childlike excitement.

"These were calls where the clients were frustrated they couldn't get the intelligence they wanted out of the system. These service calls took a long time to resolve, and many never resolved because the clients had not configured and used our software right. They hadn't understood our product and didn't understand how to use business-intelligence."

"How can you be so certain?" probed Trent.

"First we identified the calls that consumed the most time. Then we correlated those calls to the specific clients. By chance, we realized a majority of those clients weren't with us. So, next we examined their databases from our past backups and found their databases didn't have the right data, weren't configured right, and the reports didn't make sense. When we were deciding on the client-centric philosophy, I'd mentioned this phenomenon. I hadn't realized the magnitude and direct correlation to our client turnover."

"You and your engineers are pretty smart," said Hector.

"Absolutely," joined in, Trent.

"It's obvious to me from this analysis," said Hector, "if clients can't figure out how to use our software then our training is not good enough."

Venkat tried to say something, but Hector said, "I know what you're going to say. It's not just a product training issue, but a business-intelligence training issue."

Venkat shook his head in agreement.

"We need to go to the next step," continued Hector, "and map our client's work processes. Map how they should collect and use intelligence. Then our delivery resources can help them with implementing and following the process."

"This is great," said Trent excitedly. "These findings tie well with your initiative to proactively approach our top one hundred clients and evaluate their systems. It'll help us directly prevent client turnover," he concluded.

"We sure hope so," said Hector.

After they left, Trent some time thinking about all the happenings, and how he would present it all to the board at the next meeting. And, whether they would accept his thrust for Hintec.

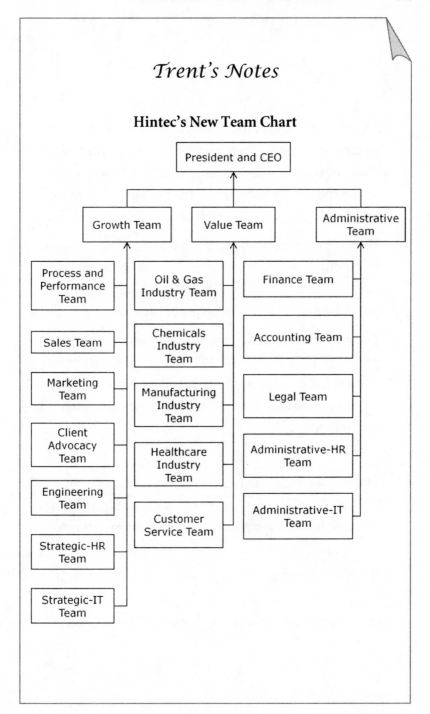

Trent's Notes

Cohegic Method Takeaways

1. The goal of organization design is to facilitate the efficient execution of work processes and not to find a place for people in the organization. The organization design must serve to reinforce the philosophies, vision, goals and strategies — cohegic flow.

2. To come up with the best, apolitical organization design, first identify the teams the organization needs, and then assign the team leaders and members. This minimizes politicking for roles and responsibilities.

3. The organization design must be team-centric and not people-centric. It must list all the teams needed even if there aren't enough people to fill all the leadership positions, and then if need be, assign one person to lead multiple teams.

Leadership Takeaways

1. The job of a leader includes coaching and mentoring his/her organization to deal with issues not in an ad-hoc manner, but in a systematic and coherent manner. A leader must not just manage but spend time developing the organization.

2. A leader has to be mindful of the unintended consequences of his actions, thinking and directions.

Chapter 14: Culture

In the evening, when Trent rang the doorbell, Watson opened the door. "Come in," he said in a cheerful voice. As they walked out to the deck, Watson said, "Martha's been busy over the summer with our grandkids. But now with them back in school, we'd like to have you folks over for dinner."

"We'd love to, thanks."

Martha walked in.

"I told Trent about the dinner."

"Good," said Martha. "I'll call Lori. Do you like fish?"

"I love fish. That'd be wonderful," said Trent.

"It's good for Watson's heart," said Martha. She smiled and left to call Lori.

Once they sat down, Trent said, "Venkat and Hector have taken ownership of the customer service problem. They're working on initiatives, analyzing the data, and finding solutions. I see no defensiveness at all."

Watson patted Trent on the back. "You have now set the right culture, the right tone. Therefore, your team members don't feel the need to be defensive. Culture, the third component of engine, is one of the most important aspects of an organization. Spirit, direction, work processes, and organization design can be perfect, yet, if Hintec doesn't develop the right culture, those elements won't matter."

"Remind me how you define culture."

"It's the collective behavior, the manner in which everyone, from the leaders to the front-line employees, think and behave. Companies often develop a culture sub-consciously, and you'll see different kinds of cultures."

"For instance?"

"Sales-oriented, operations-oriented, or finance-oriented cultures. In a sales-oriented culture, the main driver and topic of discussion is sales. Other examples include a fast-paced, energetic culture, or a slow-paced, steady culture that doesn't rock the boat too much."

"How do you relate values and culture?"

"Values describe the way an organization should conduct itself. Culture is the culmination of the actual conduct. While values are static, culture can and does change. Culture must be in-sync with the values, vision, goals and strategies."

"Cohegic flow…," once again teased Trent.

"Wouldn't have it any other way," said Watson, as he smiled. "You can't influence culture by edict. Just like kids behave according to what their parents do, not what they ask them to do, an organization takes its cues from its leaders."

Trent acknowledged with a nod.

"We can divide culture into three parts. The thinking and behavior of the CEO; the thinking and behavior of the management team, and third, the thinking and behavior of the employees. The first and second parts are similar because both the CEO and the management team members lead teams. Their guidelines are similar."

"My thinking and behavior has evolved," reflected Trent.

"I see marked changes in your conduct. As an advisor, I watch to see if what I say has an effect. I've been lucky because you listen intently and implement quickly what I recommend."

Trent smiled to acknowledge Watson's compliment.

"By implementing the Cohegic method in a logical manner you've already affected Hintec's culture."

"I see that. Hector told me he's leaving Hintec. That was the most congenial conversation I've ever had with him. His decision was not emotional but logical."

"Good progress, for you and for him. Now let's talk about one of the hardest aspects of a CEO's role — limiting politics. You must make sure your subordinates focus on working, and not on excuses, blaming others, or finding scapegoats."

Trent winced. "That's a challenge."

"In the execution phase, you shape the culture by ensuring people adhere to the values. It's similar to teaching your kids how to behave, and then, constantly reminding them to behave."

"That requires a lot of patience."

"Sure, but it's important. If you and your team don't tolerate excuses or finger pointing, Hintec will spend its time working. It's difficult to completely root out politics, but any improvement will go a long way."

"Not long ago, I was the biggest complainer," admitted Trent. "That's how I became CEO, by complaining to the board. Of course, my complaints were legitimate."

"Do you really believe you became CEO because you complained incessantly?" questioned Watson, disappointed.

"I didn't complain incessantly. I was measured, but I made sure they understood where the blame lay."

Dismayed, Watson said, "A certain amount of complaining may have influenced the board, but you're mistaken if you think that's why you became CEO. You ran the risk of the board seeing you as a non-team player. Complaining without the right reasons or excessively is the fast track to undermining a career."

"You're right. The board replaced Barry because he wasn't producing growth. If they hadn't seen that as a problem, I could've complained all I wanted. So how do I limit politics?"

"For starters, you've produced a team design based on logic and not on behind-the-door horse-trading. Second, during execution you'll have to emphasize collective accountability. No single group should celebrate or claim success if the rest of the company isn't successful. Third, you'll have to be fair."

"What do you mean by fair?"

"You can't have favorites. At the same time, you can't be afraid to make decisions or say things lest someone takes offense. You have to be direct, polite but direct. Hard to do, but if you do it without emotions and keep Hintec's interests in mind you'll do just fine. You've got to administer dispassionately and stick with the constitution."

"Constitution?"

"Hintec's spirit — the guiding principles."

Trent nodded.

"Let's discuss the second part of culture, the thinking and behavior of your management team. Much of what we discussed about the conduct and mind-set of the CEO applies to the management team members as well. But there is an additional dimension, the relationships among the management members. The employees will watch closely not only the conduct of each of them, but their interaction and dealings with each other and with you. The management team must act as a cohesive team and adhere to the values."

"I'll stay on message. I'll be fair and call out political posturing so that management can work as a team."

"Good. Let's stop here. Tomorrow we'll get into the third part, the thinking and behavior of the employees."

When Trent got back home, Lori was watching TV and eating grapes. She held the plate out for him, but he shook his head. "Everything okay? You have that lost look."

"Watson's asking me to work on reducing politics."

"That's good," she said, reducing the TV's volume.

"Yes, but if you look back, I was the one politicking to be CEO. Did I sabotage Barry?"

"I don't think so. What Maxell did was sabotaging. You weren't being Machiavellian."

He accepted her point.

"Did Martha call you about the dinner?" he asked.

"Yes, and she insisted we bring the kids."

"We need to schedule several town-hall meetings," Trent said the next morning to his assistant.

"Same format as before?" asked Amy.

"Yes, lunch included. Also invite a member of the management team to participate in each presentation."

"Okay," said Amy.

"Come in, come in" said Martha that evening, opening the door for Trent and family when he rang the doorbell.

"You're so sweet to have us over," said Lori.

"Oh, absolutely," said Martha as she picked up Catherine from the stroller.

Ethan handed Watson a framed picture of the Houston skyline.

"Oh, thank you," said Watson. He took the picture and gently touched Ethan's cheek. He assembled them around the table while Martha brought in steaming dishes.

"Mmmm, your stuffed flounder is fabulous," said Lori. "I must get your recipe."

"Sure," said Martha. She looked at Ethan. "More mac-n-cheese?" He declined but insisted on a slice of the pecan pie.

After dinner, Lori and the kids thanked Martha and returned home in time for her to put the children to bed. Trent stayed back. He and Watson helped Martha clear the table, and then walked out to the deck.

"Thanks for the dinner. It was wonderful."

"Thank you for bringing the family over." Getting right to business, Watson said, "Let's talk about the third aspect of culture, the thinking and behavior of the employees."

"Shoot."

"Culture improvement initiatives fail because companies implement them under the wrong context. The goal of improving culture isn't to create a feel-good organization, but to create a high-performance organization."

"I agree with that."

"Many leaders believe their employees lack motivation. So they employ motivational speakers, team-building exercises, social get-togethers, and creative rewards to motivate them. They increase communication through business-update e-mails, and town-hall meetings. Display the mission, vision, and values in common areas. Such initiatives, useful for creating a feel-good environment, are insufficient for creating a high-performance culture."

"I just asked Amy to restart my town-hall meetings."

"That's okay. Your challenge is to develop a culture where people don't need to be motivated. They perform to their max because they believe they can affect the results."

"And, how do you do that?"

"Three elements must exist for a high-performance culture. Employees must understand the business direction and the impact of their contributions. Two, they must have the ability to influence the direction. Three, they must receive rewards based on objective performance indicators."

"I think we've addressed the first element," said Trent. "We've clearly articulated our spirit and direction. I've shared them in emails. In the town-hall meetings I'll explain them in detail so the employees will have a better grasp."

Watson nodded. "When employees understand the business drivers, and the rationale behind the goals and strategies, they see how their day-to-day activities create value."

"Absolutely."

"Now, the second element, employees having the ability to influence the direction. I know you've been inviting employees to participate in your meetings."

"We have, and Oscar told me the employees have greatly appreciated being included."

"In addition, you and your management team need to be approachable leaders, who not only interact with employees and maintain an open-door policy, but are mentally open. You'll build a high-performance culture when you aren't afraid of employees challenging you, and you're open to them influencing you to move in a different direction."

"I've been working on becoming more open-minded."

"Giving people the ability to influence strategy is powerful because annual management retreats alone don't produce superior strategies. Strategies become superior through the implementation of good ideas that emerge spontaneously from different parts and levels of the organization."

"I'm seeing that more and more. Venkat and Hector have been generating great ideas. And, I'm sure their teams would do the same, given the opportunity and encouragement."

"Yes, they would. Now, the third element. Tying compensation to concrete indicators increases the employees' faith in controlling their own destiny, and that improves their work effort. Without objective measurement and verification, a high-performance culture is difficult to sustain."

"In addition to the things we've done what other things do we need to do to influence the right culture?"

"Employees must understand Hintec's values, and that you're serious about them. Conduct training sessions that involve role-playing to help employees learn the appropriate way to behave during challenging situations. Of course, as I've said a million times by now, nothing affects culture as much as the behavior and mindset of you and your management team."

"I think the good news is the team and I have begun to live per our values. I realize we've got a lot more room to improve."

"No human being is ever done. Speaking about improving, how're your recliner exercises?"

"I've become more regular."

"What do you experience?"

"I go through all of my thoughts, reach a point where the thoughts fade and I begin to feel sleepy. Then I go to bed."

"Wonderful. I suspect you sleep better when you do the exercise. Your mind reaches deeper sleep."

"I think you're right. I am sleeping better."

"Good to hear that. Going back to the Cohegic method, so far, you've laid the foundation, crystallized the direction, and developed the engine. The next time we meet, we'll tackle the facet of execution."

"I look forward to it."

Fran joined Trent at the town hall meeting on Friday. The lunchroom was full with fifty employees. Each had a box lunch. During the meal, Trent and Fran engaged in small talk with the employees. After everyone finished lunch, Trent stood up and explained the process he and his team had gone through. He and Fran alternated, explaining each facet and its components. Then they opened the floor for questions.

A female employee spoke up, "I don't have a question, I have a comment."

"Sure, please go ahead," said Fran.

"I want to say how much I appreciate you and Trent taking the time to come explain all these things."

"It's our pleasure, Ma'am," said Trent.

An employee raised his hand.

"Please go ahead," said Fran.

"This question's for Trent. Do you know if you're going to be our CEO going forward, you know, with all the issues we hear you've had with the board?"

"Now, wait a minute that's inappropriate," said Fran, infuriated. "Please ask questions related to what we've presented," she said firmly.

Trent motioned to her he was going to answer the question. He thought about the answer, and then said, "As far as I know, I will be the CEO."

"How do you know they're not getting ready to make a change?" challenged the employee.

The room became hush.

Trent replied calmly, "I can't speculate on it and I suggest speculating about it is no more productive than speculating whether lightening is going to strike this building."

Trent had a pained look on his face, and Fran asked him, "Should we end this meeting?"

"No," he said, continuing to think, casting his eyes at the floor, then from one side of the room to the other.

Everyone waited.

Then Trent said, "I appreciate your concern. I realize if the board made a change in the CEO position, it would cause more uncertainty in your lives."

He scanned the room, looking at their faces, and continued, "Even if there was a new CEO, I believe the new CEO would see the logic in the work we've done as part of this process. These are good decisions. The management team and many employees have jointly developed this direction. What we've presented to you today isn't my method and my decision. It represents the collective thinking of many people in this company. No one can change that or override it easily."

He paused, looked at Fran, and then said, "I'm sure you have heard in bits and pieces about the last board meeting."

Fran closed her eyes, thinking, oh, no.

"There's no point of pretending," said Trent. "Let me get it out on the table. If I don't do that, I can't see how I can have the credibility to ask you to subscribe to what we've presented. I made a mistake. I've realized it, apologized for it to my team members, and now I need to acknowledge it to you."

There was pin drop silence.

"I screwed up. Even though I'm the CEO, I'm not a superhuman, any different or any better than any of you. Just as at times, you make mistakes, I do too. I got carried away and lost control. So that we can learn from my mistake, let's put it in context. We presented to you among other things, our values. I violated our values, which were unstated then. Now, we've clearly stated them so they can serve as a guide to all of us."

He took a deep breath. "In these last two months, I've begun a transformation. I'm not done. I don't know that transforming can ever be finished because you always have more to learn and more to grow, but I've begun in earnest."

He scanned their faces again. All eyes were watching.

"I have an advisor now, who has helped me go through this personal and professional transformation. I recommend each of you to find a mentor who can help you see things about you that you can't see for yourself."

He looked at Fran. "That's all I can say at this time." He then looked back at the employees. "I have bared my soul, and I hope you'll appreciate my sincerity and transparency."

Fran motioned the meeting had ended.

The employees sitting closest to Trent stood up and came to shake his hand. Within a few minutes, the remaining employees had formed a long line, waiting to shake his hand. They told him they appreciated his openness and he had their full support.

After the meeting, Trent raced back to his office without saying anything to Fran. His eyes were moist.

That evening, he told Lori, "During the town-hall meeting today, I was overwhelmed."

"What happened?"

He shared the events of the meeting. "This is the first time I've interacted with the employees on such a personal and intimate level. Until now, they seemed distant, only a business relationship. Now, I've become one with them, as if instantaneously they've become my dear, caring friends, ready to stand beside me." He reached for her arm, looking solemn. "This experience was so intense. They changed me, not just as a CEO, but as a human being."

Lori squeezed his hand and kissed him.

He then left to see Watson. After they sat down, before Watson could start, Trent said, "I had the experience of a lifetime today."

Watson looked at Trent intently.

"At the town-hall meeting an employee challenged me."

"How did you respond?"

"Instead of being offended or defensive, I bared my soul. The interaction moved me, but more important, the employees saw me as human."

"Wow!"

"In the management team meetings, I had been including groups of ten employees, but I'm not sure I ever proactively encouraged them to participate. They raised good issues and provided good feedback, and yet it was a little distant."

Watson nodded slightly.

"At the town-hall meeting, there was no distance. We connected. I felt a part of them, not someone over them, but one of them... I'm one of them."

Watson closed his eyes, and then he got up and put his hand on Trent's shoulder. He patted his back. "I feel as if you've just scaled the peak of Mount Everest."

Trent's eyes moistened, "I feel part liberation and part joy."

"I'm proud of you. Thank you!"

"No, thank you!" said Trent emphatically.

Trent's Notes

Cohegic Method Takeaways

1. Culture is the culmination of the behavior of everyone in the organization.

2. While values are static, culture can and does change. Culture must be in-sync with the values, philosophies, vision, goals and strategies — cohegic flow.

Management and Leadership Takeaways

1. You cannot create the right culture by edict, but only through personal example.

2. In many companies, culture develops sub-consciously. A company must understand what culture it has developed by default, and then through action, not just words, migrate to the desired culture.

3. Create not a feel-good culture, but a high-performance culture where employees are self-motivated. Do so by:

   - Helping employees understand the business direction, and the contributions they make.

   - Giving employees the opportunity to influence the business direction.

   - Ensure employees receive rewards based on objective criteria.

4. A business leader must connect with employees at the personal level, not just at the business level.

Section 6: Execution & Cohesion

Chapters in the Execution and Cohesion section:

Chapter 15: Execution

Chapter 16: Cohesion

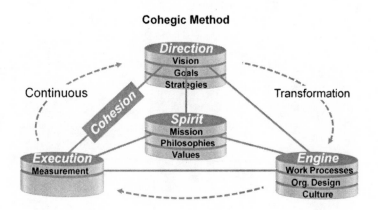

Cohegic Method

Chapter 15: Execution

On Monday, Simon called Trent. "Kathy from NAPIT Oil has finally agreed to meet with us. She was to be at a conference this week, but her trip cancelled," shared the VP of sales.

Trent looked at his calendar. "This week's difficult, but I know she's been elusive. Ask if Tuesday or Wednesday morning would be convenient for her?"

"I will," said Simon. "I'm hoping we can change her mind and convince her to use us."

Watson started that evening, "Crystallizing the spirit, direction, and engine is pointless if you don't execute. Execution, the fourth facet of the Cohegic method, is about making things happen. It's leveraging the engine to achieve the direction while staying true to the spirit." Then he grinned. "That almost sounds like the lyrics of a song."

Trent smiled, and said, "To you, is execution the same as operations?"

Watson shook his head. "Execution is bigger than operations. It covers all the actions taken across the company by all its teams: the board, management team, product team, sales team, operations team, infrastructure teams, etc."

"I get it."

"We need to consider three aspects of execution. What is the CEO's role in driving execution? What is the management team's role in driving execution? What should be the entire organization's approach to execution?"

"Okay. Let's start with my role in execution."

"For you, execution is about staying focused and following through. You must make sure things get done and get done fast by communicating clearly, following-through, and monitoring critical activities and trends."

"How do you distinguish between following-through and micro-managing?"

"It's a fine line. Following through is making sure things are happening. Micro-managing is doing it yourself or forcing people to do it only your way. Most people don't like others telling them how to do things. They're happier if you allow them to bring their creativity and preferences into play. Of course, when they're not able to produce results, then it's time to step in, ask questions, and guide them."

"I've seen effective executives ask questions inquisitively to get a pulse of what's happening," commented Trent.

"As you know, you don't get what you expect, you get what you inspect. By asking questions and understanding what's happening, you can make sure Hintec has interpreted the messages correctly and is emphasizing the right aspects to produce the results that matter."

"I thought you had said earlier I could put the system on autopilot and go play golf. Now, you're asking me to stay around and get my hands dirty."

"Very smart," said Watson, with a half-smile. "For many business leaders, execution's a trap. It becomes overwhelming and leaves them no time to think about the future or improve the organization. They're always in fire-fighting mode, moving from one crisis to another. As a leader you must make sure execution isn't just tactical but strategic as well."

Trent took notes. Then he asked, "What's my management team's role in execution?"

"Their coordination must be smooth, or Hintec won't achieve flawless execution. All their teams must jointly make sure nothing falls through the cracks. With a culture of fostering collective success, your team must ensure the interaction between all their groups is effective and efficient."

"Coordination between the teams has been a big challenge for us because the management team was never quite on the same page. From what I can see, implementing the Cohegic method has aligned them and brought them closer."

Watson pointed at Trent. "Your job is to keep the teams from drifting apart. Without your constant reminders and follow-through, team members will find fewer reasons to stay together and work together."

"I'm the designated baby-sitter," joked Trent.

"I'm afraid so," said Watson seriously. "You will prevent the development of silos only when you constantly reinforce the message of coordination and collaboration."

"What is the employees' approach to execution?"

"Discipline and a sense of urgency. Discipline is having a laser focus, allowing no distractions to impede progress. Urgency is about the entire organization pushing itself to get the job done."

"Execution's all about action."

"Yes, but you've to be careful how you push. If you push to the point where Hintec feels pressured, you'll get high performance only to a certain extent and for a limited time. If you create resonance by setting the right tempo, you could achieve super-performance. Resonance is the most important trait of good execution."

"How do I make it happen?"

"By connecting back to the spirit and direction, and reminding people they're building a school and not just laying bricks. You must get all of Hintec to buy into the vision and goals. All of Hintec must own the goals, not just the management."

"Sounds like my real work is only beginning. I need nothing short of a campaign to connect with the employees and get them all to own the goals."

"Yes, you do. And the next time, we will dive into measurement, without which you won't know how well you are executing."

The next morning, Trent and Simon headed to NAPIT Oil's office in downtown Houston for their meeting with its CIO. Kathy welcomed the duo and they started the meeting. Trent explained Hintec's client-centric approach. After he finished, Kathy said, "I like your client-centric approach. We have issues with data collection and integration, and meaningful analysis of the data. We could use your expertise."

Simon beamed. Trent was more circumspect. "Thank you," he said. "Are you going to replace GenceSoft?"

"Oh, no. I want to use Hintec in a consulting role. GenceSoft does not have the ability to help us with our internal processes and organizational challenges."

Trent shifted uncomfortably.

Without noticing Trent's reticence, Simon said, "We'll be happy to help you in any way we can. We want to begin to build a relationship with you."

Kathy looked at Trent. "You don't seem too sure."

Simon turned to look at Trent. Seeing Trent's expression, he dropped his shoulders.

"I'm delighted you like our client-centric approach," said Trent, "and are offering us a chance to work with you. But, we're not a purely consulting company. Our client-centric services are closely tied to our product."

Simon squirmed.

Kathy said, "I appreciate your position. I can't replace GenceSoft's business-intelligence module with Hintec... at least not for a year because we've already paid for a year's support. Let's talk next year."

As they walked back to the car, Simon didn't say anything. Trent could tell Simon was upset. As they drove off, Trent said, "It was really tempting to take Kathy's offer."

"But we have to stay true to our philosophy," said Simon sarcastically.

"That's right," said Trent as he smiled at Simon's petulance. "It's a slippery slope. If we take purely consulting gigs, it'll send a confusing message and completely undermine our product. I understand you feel this would've allowed us to get our foot in the door and we could get our product in later."

"You bet, I do," said Simon, strongly.

"But think about the time our delivery resources would spend learning GenceSoft's product. That'd be a waste of time and distracting to our delivery resources. Also, our new pricing, which I have told you our clients like, does not price our client-centric services separately but as part of our annual fees."

Simon sighed.

"Execution is about consistent thinking and delivery. I need your help to make sure our sales execution is cohesive with our strategies and philosophies," reinforced Trent.

When he got back to the office, Trent stopped by Amy's office. "Would you check if Hector and Venkat are available for a short meeting later in the afternoon today?"

Late in the afternoon, Hector and Venkat walked in.

"Hi, Trent," they said as they took their seats.

He greeted them, and then said, "Simon and I met with a prospect this morning. It reminded me of your initiative to visit with our top one hundred clients and proactively evaluate their systems. What have you found?"

"It's been only two weeks when we first approached you with the idea," said Hector. "Venkat's engineers who handle the Tier 3 calls have taken the lead to contact the clients."

Trent looked at Venkat.

"So far, we have approached fifteen clients to schedule their systems evaluation," answered Venkat. "And, currently we are evaluating the systems of five clients."

"Good. How much time will we spend on each client?"

"Between ten to twenty hours," replied Venkat.

"I'm interested in finding out what challenges our clients are facing. The CIO of NAPIT Oil described to us this morning the challenges they're facing." Trent paused. A small light bulb went off in his mind. "Why didn't we involve Simon in this initiative? One of the tenets of execution is to ensure good coordination and collaboration among the teams."

Venkat struggled a little bit. "We'd be happy to have Simon involved. But these are existing clients and this initiative came about as a result of the client retention strategy."

"I understand what you're saying," said Trent. "You thought this was only a client retention issue. I'm not picking on you. Even I didn't think of mentioning that we should include Simon when you'll first suggested the initiative."

"Trent is right," said Hector. "If we involve the sales team, maybe we'll discover opportunities to sell our clients more licenses as we understand their issue. Then this initiative could be more than just a defensive move."

"Exactly," said Trent.

"I see it," said Venkat. "We should have the engineers and the salespeople work together to understand each of these client's situation." Venkat paused, rubbing his forehead. "We should take a second look at the work process design for client retention, and factor in the collaboration between sales, engineering, and customer service."

"Thank you for saying that, Venkat," said Trent. "Updating the work process design is the right way to systematically implement what we just discussed. That way we know, it'll be executed well and consistently."

That evening as Watson and Trent headed out to the deck they heard thunder. It wasn't raining but they decided to sit inside in Watson's home-office.

"You can't execute effectively or efficiently unless you measure," started Watson. "You won't know precisely what's happening and what's working."

"I agree. We must measure and monitor the strategic progress and the operational performance."

"Measuring will add teeth to your goals and strategies and reinforce the strategic message in the organizational psyche."

"The problem with measurement is that it will increase the administrative burden," pushed back Trent. "Collecting data, streamlining, and reporting are non-trivial activities. People will resist this added work."

"You can solve that problem by introducing only a few simple metrics to begin with. Also, if you have too many metrics, people won't know which are critical."

"How do we keep the metrics simple?"

"Start with subjective and qualitative. As Hintec understands metrics and its capability to measure improves, you can transition to add quantitative and objective metrics."

"What's the next step?"

"You need to develop three simple plans: a three-year plan, a twelve-month plan, and a quarterly plan."

"What should we include in the plans?"

"For the three-year plan, include the vision components, and their associated metrics and targets. Similarly, for the twelve-month plan include the twelve-month goals, and the related metrics and targets. For the quarterly plan, do the same, except you still have to define your quarterly objectives."

"That sounds straightforward. Should we look at our vision to see which metrics we need as part of our three-year plan?"

"Sure, let's do it," said Watson.

Trent took out the vision statement. They both studied it.

"To measure our client-centric vision," said Trent, "our clients must be willing to give us written testimonials categorically stating Hintec created significant value, and rate their experience of using Hintec as excellent."

"What would your target be?"

"Let me think… at least 90% of clients should acknowledge that Hintec created significant value."

Watson smiled.

"That's aggressive based on where we stand now, but that's our vision. We must be there in three years."

"Okay," said Watson, agreeing with Trent. "Now for your growth vision, you can measure it in two ways; growth in the number of upper-tier accounts, and growth in the ratio of upper-tier revenues versus total revenues."

"I like those two metrics, they'll remind us to stay focused on our upper-tier philosophy. Right now only 60% of our revenues come from accounts that are greater than $500,000. The target should be 75% in one year, 85% in two years, and 100% in three years. What do you think about those targets?"

"I'm okay with your targets. As you get data from execution, derive better benchmarks and adjust them."

"That covers the three-year plan," observed Trent. "Turning to the twelve-month plan, what should be our metrics to measure the twelve-month goal of increasing sales effectiveness?"

"Ah, that's an important and yet tricky goal."

"Currently we measure sales success ratio and sales cycle-time," shared Trent.

"They're good indicators, but they're lagging indicators. They tell you how things went, after the fact, after the deals are done. You need to supplement them with leading metrics that portend future results. One such critical metric is the quality of opportunities in the pipeline."

"How do we measure opportunity quality?"

"Look for cues from your strategy. In your sales effectiveness strategy, you've identified several elements such as mitigating the risk associated with your solution, developing an internal executive-level champion. The hypothesis is that these elements will improve the sales-success ratio and cycle time. You should measure to prove or disprove that hypothesis. Do opportunities with a higher rating in one strategic element have a higher success ratio? If you see a pattern, you'd have discovered a top sales driver."

"And, if we find that a strategic element doesn't affect the success ratio, then it'd be time to replace that factor in the strategy with something else. Measuring these elements will allow us to fine-tune our sales effectiveness strategy."

Watson smiled. "That's the purpose of measurement. The quality of opportunities is a good leading indicator. You'll be able to use it along with the volume of opportunities in the pipeline to predict more accurately how sales will perform in the future."

Trent smiled. "That will make the board happy."

"Metrics is an interesting topic. We could talk about it for a long time but let's not. As you cycle through the dynamic facets of direction, engine and execution, your metrics will become more sophisticated and insightful."

The next day, Trent discussed the three-year plan with his team. He finished saying, "Since the twelve-month plan can be developed similarly, would some of you like to complete it offline and present it to the rest of us in the next meeting?"

"That's a good idea," said Fran. "I can lead that effort."

"I volunteer to help Fran," said Venkat. "I can develop some template graphs to go along with the metrics."

The following morning Fran and Venkat presented their twelve-month plan. After they finished, Trent said, "As I heard you go through all the twelve-month goals and their metrics and targets, I kept thinking about the metrics for client retention."

"Do you not like what we have now, measuring client turnover?" asked Fran.

"Client turnover is necessary, but one, it is a lagging indicator, and two, it is internally focused."

"Internally focused, how?" asked Fran.

"It's our view of the world."

"You mean we need a metric from the client's perspective," said Venkat.

"Yes," said Trent gesturing with his hand. "What would be a client-centric metric?"

"It's their view of what we're delivering," said Venkat. "How many outstanding customer issues they see having with us? How much value they perceive in our product?"

Trent beamed. "Yes," he said energetically.

"This is great," said Venkat getting excited too. "These metrics go hand-in-hand with our initiative to proactively approach clients."

"Those are good metrics," said Fran. "And, they're both leading metrics. They'll tell us what type of client turnover we could expect in the future."

Everyone smiled. It was as if the entire team was performing in an orchestra, working in unison and cueing off each other.

As Trent was getting ready to leave at the end of the day, Oscar came to see him. "We may be at a tipping point. The interest among employees in the mission, vision, strategies, really picked up after your last town-hall."

"That's great news."

Oscar nodded. "You had emailed the employees the mission, vision, but I think they had read it only cursorily. Now, several employees went back and reread that email, and have asked me questions about it. They're beginning to get plugged in."

"Thanks, Oscar. Thanks a bunch."

In the next meeting, Trent and his team identified the quarterly objectives to execute in the next quarter. When they finished, Trent recorded them on the white board.

"Let me assign an importance ranking to the quarterly objectives," said Trent. When he was done, he said, "All of the objectives seem a 10 to me."

"That doesn't make sense," observed Hector.

"I guess they're all important," said Trent. "We need to accomplish all of them this quarter."

"Instead of ranking them based on importance," offered Venkat, "we should rank them based on the sequencing order or shorter-term priority. The order in which we wish to execute, similar to the sequencing of software development tasks we do in project management."

"That would make sense," said Trent.

Hector wasn't sure. "Isn't importance and sequencing order the same?"

"No," said Venkat. "An objective may be important, but we may not be able to work on it until we complete some other objective. To rank based on importance makes sense when the time-frame is longer. For shorter time-frames, sequencing is far more relevant."

"Thank you, professor Venkat," said Hector. Everyone laughed.

Looking at Trent, Hector said, "Have you noticed all these objectives relate to Hintec's strategic thrust?"

"That's because we looked at our goals hierarchy to develop them," said Trent. "I guess we should add objectives that concern our day-to-day, routine operations and activities."

"Yes," said Hector. "If we do that, all the employees will be able to see how they individually contribute to at least one or more quarterly objectives."

Satisfied, Trent said, "Adding our operational objectives will provide a complete picture of what Hintec must execute strategically and operationally."

That evening Trent showed Watson the three plans. "What do you think," he asked.

After he looked at it, Watson said, "Looks good. Now, you must train and coach the supervisors to cascade the quarterly objectives down to the objectives for every employee. Let me restate that. Supervisors must develop their own objectives, and then work with each employee to develop the employee's objectives. It would start with the supervisor reemphasizing the spirit and the direction, and then answering any questions the employee may have."

"The quarterly objectives relate to what the employees must accomplish, but they don't address how they should do it."

"Good point," said Watson. "I'd add a quarterly objective, which states that Hintec must imbibe its values.

Now, each supervisor can guide their subordinates on the personal objectives they must develop to embody the values."

"Very good," said Trent.

"This interaction between the supervisors and their subordinates regarding objectives will pave the way for quarterly evaluations. Frequent performance evaluations lead to greater objectivity," said Watson. "Performance feedback provided only once a year is subjective because it's difficult for supervisors to remember all the facts and be specific."

"I'm concerned reviewing quarterly is too often. We review annually and it takes a significant amount of time."

"This is the heart of execution," emphasized Watson animatedly. "If the supervisors don't discuss and give specific guidance to every employee about what they must do differently each quarter, then what hope do you have of seeing your strategy executed? There's nothing more important that requires the time and attention of the supervisors."

Trent's eyes widened. "You're right. I want every employee to stop and think every quarter, what they're doing to contribute to the strategy and what they need to do better compared to the previous quarter. We'll be redefining our execution plan and updating our strategic plan every quarter based on what's working and what isn't, so the employees need to take note."

Watson smiled. "Now you're talking. Cohegic flow, remember."

In the next management meeting, Trent started, "We now have the three-year, one-year and quarterly plans. Let me know if you see an objective or metric that we need to rephrase."

Several team members nodded.

Trent looked around the table, and slapping the table said, "It's time to execute! I'll accelerate the town-hall meetings and work with Oscar to develop a training program for all supervisors. Also, Oscar and I will aggressively prepare ourselves to fill the various roles."

Trent stopped and looked around the table. "This has been an incredible experience for me," he reflected. "I can't thank each one of you enough for helping me."

"We thank you, too," said Oscar and the others nodded. "You've helped Hintec immensely. I'm sure the board will appreciate your efforts."

"Speaking about which," said Trent, "the board meeting comes up in three weeks. I really hope they appreciate our cohegic approach."

Trent's Notes

Cohegic Method Takeaways

1. Execution covers all the actions taken across the company by all its teams: the board, management, product team, sales team, operations team, etc.

2. Execution is leveraging the engine to achieve the direction while staying true to the spirit — cohegic flow.

3. Measurement adds teeth to the goals and strategies, and reinforces the strategic message — cohegic flow.

4. Rank quarterly objectives based on a sequencing order /shorter-term priority. Ranking vision and goals on importance makes sense because the timeframe is longer. For shorter timeframes, sequencing is more relevant.

Management and Leadership Takeaways

1. To execute effectively, a business leader must monitor, measure and follow-through. Execution is about discipline and a sense of urgency, across the board.

2. Executing strategy effectively requires providing employees regular feedback. Annual performance feedback is not frequent enough; supervisors must provide feedback quarterly.

3. Resonance is an important trait of excellent execution.

4. Companies often design metrics influenced from an internal perspective. Design metrics from the perspective of the clients.

Trent's Notes

THREE-YEAR PLAN

Three-year Vision (Relative Importance - Max: 10)	Metrics	Targets
CLIENT-CENTRIC VISION (10): Become fully client-centric; Build client-centric capabilities and deliver successfully	% of clients willing to acknowledge significant value created	90% of clients
	% of clients rate Hintec experience as excellent	90% of clients
GROWTH VISION (8): Be significantly larger in revenues; # of clients; engagement size	Total annual revenues	First year - $240 Million; Second Yr - $290 Million; Third Yr - $350 Million;
	% of revenues from upper-tier accounts versus total revenues	First Year - 75%; Second Yr - 85%; Third Yr - 100%;
	Number of new upper-tier clients	To be determined
	Minimum engagement size (in recurring annual revenues)	> $1 Million by end of third year
RECOGNITION VISION (7): Be considered as a premier upper-tier BI provider	To be determined	To be determined

QUARTERLY PLAN

Quarterly Objectives (Priority - Max:10)	Metrics	Quarterly Targets
Roll out spirit, direction, and engine across Hintec (10)	Feedback from employees	90% respond they understand spirit and direction
Fill key positions (10)	% of Positions Filled	50% of the positions filled
Visit with upper-tier clients to strengthen relationships (10)	Progress made	50% of the upper-tier clients visited
Update marketing collaterals to reflect client-centric approach (10)	Progress made	100% completed
Put new sales process into effect; Retrain sales people (9)	Progress made	100% completed
Continue to generate new sales (8)	New sales revenues	Meet sales target
Continue to deliver excellent customer service (8)	Customer satisfaction rating	80% favorable rating
Implement product enhancements (8)	Progress made	Functional list developed
Build and nurture the right culture (8)	Internal employee survey; External survey	70% of response is favorable
Develop interaction map among teams to facilitate flawless coordination (7)	Progress made	100% completed
Develop IT System to capture client-centric information (7)	Progress made	100% completed
Continue to ensure good operational performance across Finance, Accounting, HR and IT (7)	Management team satisfaction	90% of management team members satisfied

Chapter 16: Cohesion

"Today, we discuss the facet that holds all the static and moving parts together," Watson started their deck chat. "Actually, we've been talking about cohesion all along."

"I know," said Trent teasing Watson. "I've repeated cohegic flow a million times."

Watson gave him a playful look. "The cohesion facet has several dimensions. First, Hintec's engine and execution must align with its direction and spirit. Second, the board, upper management, middle management, and front-line employees must share a consistent mindset. Third, your suppliers and service providers must be in-sync with Hintec's needs. Fourth, be sure the expectations and perceptions of customers and prospects align with what Hintec stands for and can deliver, and finally, ensure the community and Hintec align with and support each other."

"That's a tall order."

"It sure is. As a leader, you must tie everything together. You have the vantage point"

"I understand that completely. You've engrained it in my being."

"That's good," said Watson, nodding his head vigorously. "You'll find people tend to be like geese, heading in different directions because of differing interpretations and personal preferences. You have to remind everyone all the time to stay on the course."

Trent added his analogy, "Hintec is more like a fast train than ducks or geese. I realize it's important for me to ensure all the boxcars keep speeding along the same track."

"I like your analogy. Cohesion isn't about rigidity, but about structural integrity. Unless there's some aspect to tie down all the moving parts, you risk disintegration."

"In our very first meetings, you told me the most important thing a leader does is maintain focus."

Watson smiled broadly. "Yes, and cohesion is ensuring focus by sticking with the message. The role of a business leader is akin to the role of a lobbyist, perpetually lobbying the spirit and direction message. As the CEO, you must be the glue to hold Hintec together."

"I will. And, I'll ask my team to do the same."

"Yes, of course. A management team is an extension of the CEO and must emulate the CEO's thrust and behavior. Let's extend that further. Every mid-level manager too must be an extension of you, and an advocate of the spirit and direction. When all the leaders in Hintec are cohesive in their thinking and actions, you'll have a powerful Hintec, performing to its fullest potential."

"That'll be a wonderful day," said Trent. "We'll be cohesive, and yet flexible and agile because we'll have all the flexibility to change our strategies and tactics."

"That's exactly right."

"How would the teams and sub-teams in Hintec fully use this method?"

"In two ways. First, they will develop mission, philosophies, and values that are specific to their team."

"So, as an example, the engineering team may crystallize philosophies regarding the technologies they use, or the way in which they develop and test their software?" asked Trent.

"Yes, that's a good example. Second, the teams will develop their goals and strategies to support the overall corporate goals and strategies."

"That makes sense," said Trent. "If all the teams adopt this method at their level, to influence how they did work, it will improve cohesion."

"Yes and that way they will have a greater buy-in for the method and a better understanding of its facets. Let's talk about cohesion with the board members. Have you stayed in touch with Cedric?"

"Yes, I've been calling him at least every two weeks, and he's happy with our direction and progress."

"What about the other board members?"

"Cedric advised me to wait until closer to the next board meeting and then update them on our progress."

"I recommend you start having those conversations and get their buy-in. Build a coalition of board members who'll support you. If you do that before the meeting, you won't be surprised or blind-sided at the meeting. You'll have determined the outcome of the meeting even before it starts."

"I'll start working on it immediately."

"I'm really glad to see that you and your team have gone through the facets in time for you to make your presentation at the next board meeting. I sure hope the board likes your effort, commitment, and direction."

"We shall know soon," said Trent, raising his eyebrows.

The night before the board meeting, Lori and Trent were in the bedroom. Lori had her book and Trent lay on his back.

She looked at him and asked, "Are you prepared for the board meeting?"

Trent sat up. "I feel confident. I've talked with most of the board members and apprised them of what we've done. They were supportive and encouraging."

"What about Cedric?" asked Lori, wanting to know where the Chairman stood.

"Cedric is supportive. In fact, I asked him to present an overview of what we've accomplished. I was happy he agreed. It'll ensure the board's enthusiastic endorsement."

Lori smiled. "How's the rest of Hintec feeling?"

"Great. The town-hall meetings have allowed me to connect with the employees and bring them into the fold. I've also involved mid-level managers in the presentations, which has gone really well."

"Let me start this meeting," said Cedric at the October board meeting. "Trent and his team have accomplished a great deal in the last three months. They have a new bold direction. It'll help Hintec deliver sustainable growth."

Trent smiled.

Cedric continued, "I'm proud of the inclusive and transparent manner in which the initiative has unfolded. The management members and employees have enthusiastically bought in, and the process has energized them."

Cedric looked around the table and said, "I understand Trent visited with most of you individually to update you and explain the components. I congratulate Trent and his team on a job well done."

Most everyone in the room nodded in agreement. Cedric looked at Trent and said, "It's all yours."

"Thank you, Cedric. I'm grateful for your endorsement. Your encouragement has meant a lot to me and has kept me going during the difficult periods of implementing this method."

Trent looked at the board members. "This method is an ongoing process, a continuous transformation. We'll cycle through the dynamic facets, and with each cycle, our thinking, focus and efforts will become more effective, efficient and productive."

In a tone undercutting Trent's enthusiasm, John Summers, the board member representing the private equity investors, RiverRock Funds, said, "I appreciate the motivational speech."

Everyone turned toward John.

"As I review the package you've distributed, I'm shocked," said John. "This is a significant expense, not counting the loss of productivity from engaging your entire management team and scores of employees in this initiative. Oh, and you said, we're going to keep doing this indefinitely. I guess you must not be a big shareholder."

Trent looked scornful. He reminded himself to stay calm and relaxed before answering. "John, it's easy to fall in the trap of knowing the cost of everything and the value of nothing. We're building for the future, investing in Hintec so it can yield bigger returns for you and our other investors."

"I sit on a lot of boards and hear enough stories about investing for the future. That's all they are, good stories. RoundRock isn't interested in building companies for the next decade. We look for quicker returns in the short to mid-term. Drive sales, drive efficiencies, so you can maximize profits. Stop dreaming about the future and focus on fixing the present."

Trent looked around the table to gauge reactions.

John pressed on, "I read your new org chart and see Hector your COO hasn't been assigned to lead the value team. I thought in the last board meeting, we made it clear we don't want you to fire Hector. In fact, he should be COO and President, so he can counter-balance your pie-in-the-sky schemes."

Cedric jumped in, "Wait a minute, John. I don't think…"

"Cedric, I think I should answer John's questions," interrupted Trent, in a confident tone. "He's directed them to me and I don't want to hide from his questions."

Cedric gave a brief smile and leaned back in his chair.

Looking at John, Trent continued, "First, it's most important to have cohesion between the board and the management team. By cohesion, I mean alignment around the mission, values, philosophies and vision. I hear you. I do. And I respect what you're saying, but for us to be on the same page, we must put things in context."

Trent took a deep breath. "What you've described is a valid philosophy, only it's different from the one the management team and I have developed over the last three months. Mind you, we didn't develop our philosophies and vision without due consideration. We took our time to consider all the angles, and then, through open discussion, we arrived at our conclusion. I'll admit the conclusions weren't always born out of unanimous consensus, but in the time since, I promise you the entire management team including Hector is 100% behind what we've developed."

John begun to say something, but Trent cut him off. "Please let me finish. Your proposition to focus on profits is what Hintec had done for the last few years. When the board hired me as the CEO, the mandate was to produce growth. With the help of an advisor, I realized Hintec's core philosophies weren't oriented toward growth. I'm sure, we could grow somewhat, staying with our old philosophy of being product-centric, but it runs against the grain of our product and our industry. Hence, it limits us."

Gaining greater confidence and sureness in his voice, Trent said, "The philosophies of client-centric and the focus on upper-tier, makes the most sense for Hintec. I can't guarantee our decisions are correct, but I can guarantee we've reached them through logical and sound reasoning. We didn't base our decisions on emotions or gut, which I may submit with all due respect, you're doing now."

John frowned.

Trent continued without relenting, "We're going into this with our eyes open. If we're wrong, we'll have no hesitation admitting it and changing course. If we've made a mistake, will that cost Hintec? Yes, it will, but I'm sure there isn't one great organization on earth that hasn't made mistakes. As long as we're vigilant, recognize our mistakes, and change course in a timely fashion, I guarantee we'll do great."

Trent paused and looked around. John was still seething.

"Let me also address the elephant in the room, the last board meeting," said Trent. "I let my emotions take control. I have learned and grown tremendously since then."

Several board members nodded.

"As far as Hector is concerned, he offered to leave, explaining he didn't have the interest or skills to serve in the new client-centric Hintec. I respect his reasons and his decision. It made sense. It's reasonable to expect that as you create new roles, you may not find all the talent in-house to serve in those roles."

Cedric nodded.

"Hintec is finally getting its act-together," continued Trent. "In the last three months, it's gone through an incredible transformation; and yet, we're only beginning. I hope you can see that, respect it and join us in making Hintec a huge and sustained success."

"I wish you all the best," said John with a smirk.

After the meeting ended, several board members, including Cedric, came up and commended Trent on his confidence, demeanor and response to John.

Cedric said to Trent, "I have discussed this with the other board members. We want to grant stock to Watson as a thank you for his valuable guidance and advice. I'll email the details to you."

"Thank you so much," said Trent.

Trent shared the events of the board meeting with Watson. "I must thank you, Watson. Your advice to build a coalition before the meeting was invaluable. At the board meeting where I lost face, I was all by myself. None of the board members said anything to support me. It was different today. Even though John pushed hard, it was clear from the body language of the other board members that their vote was with me. John found himself isolated in the end."

"Excellent. Well done."

"Your message of cohesion with the board members was right on the money," concluded Trent. "To thank you for your guidance and advice, the board has decided to grant you stock in Hintec."

"What? I hadn't asked for anything."

"I know, but I can't thank you enough for what you have done for me and for Hintec."

Watson smiled. "Well, thank you."

Three weeks passed quietly. Then on a Monday afternoon, Cedric came to visit Trent. After they exchanged pleasantries, Cedric said, "Hintec and RoundRock are parting ways."

"Really?" Trent tried his best not to react, but gave in and smiled at the news of not having John Summers on the board anymore.

"Yes. I felt it was the right decision. We've attracted a new investor, Jupiter Ventures, who are more aligned with our plans for Hintec."

"That sounds wonderful," said Trent all energized.

"There's this issue…," said Cedric struggling. "They're insisting on bringing in an executive they know, as CEO."

Trent turned pale. He looked at Cedric searchingly.

"I'm sorry," said Cedric, trying to escape the gaze. "I've been very pleased with what you've done, and the conviction you demonstrated in the board meeting. Knowing you followed a logical and coherent method gives me great confidence in the future of Hintec."

Trent could hardly hear Cedric's words. His palms wet with sweat, he looked away at the window.

"I haven't decided on my final answer to Jupiter ventures. I'd like to visit with the management team before I do that. Can we arrange a meeting tomorrow morning?"

"Sure," said Trent. Barely able to get words out, he added, "I'll sit out of that meeting, so they can freely express what they feel."

"None of them is shy. I want you to be there because I still see a role for you at Hintec."

Cedric left. Trent's emotions were raging.

"I'm being replaced as CEO," Trent shared with Lori, as soon as he stepped in the house.

"Why?" she asked, shocked. "You worked so hard to change yourself. You've put Hintec on the right path, reinvented it... transformed it. How can they do that? I don't believe this."

Trent looked lost. "It's not performance related," he rued. "Cedric says he liked what I've accomplished. But we're bringing in new investors and they want their guy to be CEO."

Lori shook her head.

Trent took a deep breath and sat down on the couch. "I had wished John Summers would go away. Sometimes, you've to be careful what you wish for."

"I'll fix dinner, so you can go see Watson."

"I'm not going."

She rubbed his shoulders, and then gave him a tight hug.

Trent tried to do the recliner exercise that night before he planned to go to bed. It did him no good. His mind raged uncontrollably. He questioned what he could have done different. He felt cheated.

It was well past mid-night before he got up and lay down on the bed. It was a while before he fell asleep.

Cedric started the meeting with the management team the next morning, "After the last board meeting, John Summers' private equity firm, and we, the board, realized the fit isn't very good. So, Hintec and RiverRock have mutually decided to part ways."

"So, what happens now? How does it affect us?" asked Hector.

"Good question," said Cedric. "We've lined up another firm, Jupiter Ventures. They're reputable, large enough to provide stability, and agree with our philosophies and direction."

"Great," said several members.

"However, the challenge is they have a precondition. They want to bring in their own person as CEO," said Cedric dropping the bombshell. "But before I agreed, I wanted to run that by you. The last time, we changed CEOs, several of you complained about the lack of transparency, which is now one of our values."

There was a minute of silence as everyone digested the news.

"You've got to do what's right for Hintec," said Fran.

"That's right," said Cedric.

Fran looked at Trent and then looked at Cedric. "Having Trent continue to lead Hintec is the right thing."

Cedric looked caught off-guard. Fran continued, "No one understands the philosophies and direction we've adopted better than Trent. He has put his soul into it and is the one who can take it to fruition."

"I second that," said Hector.

"We're considerably lucky to have found Jupiter Ventures so quickly," explained Cedric. "We can't afford to lose them, and they're pretty insistent."

"I agree with what Fran has said," weighed in Oscar.

Simon and Venkat looked at each other. "We do too," they said joining in.

"You need to take a hard stance," insisted Fran. "We've learned from Trent about making sure all aspects of our business are cohesive. The board needs to ensure cohesion as much as, or even more than the management team. We've communicated the new thrust to all the employees. Replacing Trent will undermine the whole effort, and violate cohesion."

Cedric ended the meeting, realizing he was in a tight spot. He hadn't expected such a strong endorsement of Trent from the team.

After the meeting, Trent went to see Fran.

"You don't have to thank me," she said. "I didn't do it for you. I did it for Hintec. It's the right thing."

It was late in the evening. Trent was getting ready to leave when Cedric walked into his office and closed the door.

"Jupiter was not pleased with my inflexibility," said Cedric. "They saw it as my emotional attachment to you. But for now, they've agreed to disagree. They'll still come on board, and won't insist on replacing you. At least, not for six to twelve months. That's the best I could do. "

Trent let out a sigh of relief. "I can't thank you enough," he said. "I've greatly appreciated your support and encouragement throughout this process."

"You've taught us how important it is to be cohegic. Now you need to execute your plans, and deliver solidly and rapidly."

"I will with full force. Thanksgiving and Christmas are coming up, but I'm not going to slow down. Oscar and the team have already helped me identify candidates. The holidays will be a great opportunity to make progress on filling these key roles. We'll visit with our existing clients and explain our new client-centric philosophy, and we'll try to win back some of our lost clients, especially the high profile ones, like Zucor and Wesley Chemicals."

"Okay," said Cedric as he got up.

"Cedric," called out Trent, as Cedric turned to leave.

"Are you in a difficult place with Jupiter Ventures on my accord?"

"I'll be fine. Though, I'm sure at some point they'll claim a pound of my flesh."

"What a year it's been," said Trent to Watson when he took over a gift basket, the week before Christmas. "I wouldn't have made it without you. I can't thank you enough."

"You're welcome. I'm glad you were able to stabilize and turn the situation around. How're you progressing?"

"The team and I've worked hard on accomplishing the quarterly objectives. I've just extended an offer to a consulting company executive to lead our value team. Some of the board and management team members participated in the interviews and were happy with the choice."

"That's good."

"Hector's found a new job and is leaving amicably. I asked him to reconsider but he really likes the job he found. After interviewing multiple candidates, the management team and I agreed Jose Hernandez, the director of customer service whom Hector recommended, is best to fill his shoes."

Watson smiled.

"Simon returned to selling full-time. We hired a sales VP from a competitor. I've made sure the new sales VP has interest and skills in managing the team and the sales process."

"I'm happy with your progress."

"I'm still struggling to find someone to lead the growth team, someone who has a background in strategic development and enough experience in operations, to be able to lead the process, sales, marketing and engineering teams."

In the second week of January, Trent attended the annual meeting of one of Houston's business associations. As he was looking for his name badge, he spied the name badge of Randy Vesco, CEO of their former client, Wesley Chemicals.

A man dressed in a grey suit stepped up beside him, picked up the badge and attached it to his jacket. Trent attached his own badge quickly and extended his hand.

"Hi, I'm Trent Wertheimer, president and CEO of Hintec."

"Good to meet you," said Randy shaking Trent's hand. "What does Hintec do?"

"We're a business-intelligence company."

"Ah, very good," said Randy.

"Are you involved with this association?" asked Trent.

"Yes, I'm on the board this year. We've not been in the public limelight, and we've decided to change that."

"What's driving the shift?"

"We're a $12 billion company, but we've decided to be more aggressive, given the economic conditions. I've asked my management team to get involved in the community. It'll help us build stronger relations with customers and prospects, potential talent, even service providers."

Trent smiled.

"Why are you smiling?" asked Randy.

"Hintec is a service provider and you just provided me the best opening. May I ask, as you pursue growth, what business-intelligence tools do you plan to use to help you gain the insights you need to make superior decisions?"

"We used to use a business-intelligence software package, I can't remember the name. Our IT department couldn't build a strong enough business case for us to spend millions of dollars on it."

Looking at the rest of the people, Randy said, "Everyone's headed into the ballroom for lunch."

"If you're sitting at an open table, may I join you?"

"I'm not, but let's see if there's an empty seat."

Randy located a seat for Trent and the two men sat down.

"Thank you, for your graciousness."

"I wanted to continue our discussion. Where were we?"

"You threw out the BI software you were using."

"Yes, we did. We couldn't see the value. The reports our IT department produced contained information we already knew. What a waste of time."

"I can tell you why that happened," offered Trent. "The IT department didn't work with you to understand your business imperatives. So they couldn't identify the specific information you weren't already receiving."

"That's right. I suspect we're not capturing the relevant data to begin with. It's difficult to generate a report on data we don't have."

"Well, there's a solution," advised Trent. "Your business-intelligence team must work closely with the executive team, determine which information's critical, find ways to capture that data as a part of operations, analyze the data, and finally present it to the executive team, who can then make better decisions."

"That sounds wonderful. Can your company do that?"

"Yes, sir. We can now."

"What do you mean, now?" asked Randy raising an eyebrow.

"We've spent the last year transforming Hintec from a product-centric company to a customer-centric company. Our focus is no longer just to sell our product; instead we've geared to use our product to help our customers make faster and better, strategic and operational decisions."

"That makes sense," said Randy.

"That change in philosophy has rewired our company. As a result, today, we can effectively address your needs." Trent paused, and then continued evenly, "We couldn't do that a year ago when we lost your account."

"Excuse me."

"Yes sir. Wesley Chemicals used our business-intelligence software. Thanks in part to losing you, we have reinvented our company. We understood the mistakes we were making. We have developed ourselves as a client-centric company. I can appreciate you may be wary of trusting us again, but have you ever made mistakes as a company and learned from those mistakes?" He took a deep breath and continued, "If you hear us out, I promise it'll be worth your time."

"We've made mistakes and we've learned," said Randy. Then he laughed and shook his head in disbelief. "You sound sincere about having rediscovered yourself," he said. "I'll give you a chance, if only because I'd like to hear the whole story."

Trent grinned in triumph.

That evening, Trent shared the incident with Watson.

"I'm happy for you," said Watson. "Listening to clients and connecting with their needs are the core tenets of cohesion."

"I hope we're able to sign them up again."

"I'm sure you will."

"Thank you for your advice to be involved with community organizations. At another business luncheon, I met an experienced executive, Chad Brunson, who recently stepped down as the president of a $50 million business unit after the parent corporation sold the unit. I'm having the board and the management team, talk to him about the role of the leader of the growth team."

"Good."

"We've also hired a VP of Marketing, Peter Avon," shared Trent. "Once he came on-board, I shared with him our struggles with Maxell, our previous VP of marketing. Peter has made me appreciate the value of a well thought out and consistent look-n-feel across our marketing collaterals. And, the value of increasing our brand profile through various means including social media. Maxell was attempting to do the same, but because we didn't connect I never did appreciate his point-of-view."

"Does Peter appreciate your hard focus on ensuring marketing ROI?"

"Yes, he does. I know I was quite forceful about that with Maxell. Peter appreciates that marketing must drive the sales engine. So we are on the same page."

It was the end of February before Trent made another visit to see Watson.

"Hey, stranger! How've you been? I haven't seen you in weeks," said Watson.

"Sorry. You're right, I think we met six weeks ago."

"How're things going?"

"Quite well. I'm extremely busy. There's an unending list of items to make happen, but we're making good progress. The sales pipeline looks great. George, the new VP of sales is pushing hard on the sales team, and they're responding."

"What type of deals are they going after?"

"Good deals, high end."

"Are you watching the quality of the deals?"

"I haven't, but George is monitoring closely."

"Do you know that or is that your hope?"

"Well, as part of the new org chart, the VP sales reports to Chad, the leader of the growth team. When both of them came on board, I explained the sales process, and the metrics we want tracked. My interaction with sales is now lesser, as I've delegated. I'm consumed by all the other things. I do know the sales numbers. They look good."

"But, you don't know the quality of deals in the pipeline, and whether salespeople are leveraging the sales drivers."

"You're right, I suppose," conceded Trent.

"What happened to the sales metrics you were going to track?"

"We modified our sales automation software to track them, but we've not had enough data to discern a pattern."

"So, what has been keeping you busy?" asked Watson.

"Hiring for one. We've been filling the positions. I've taken a personal interest in recruiting because finding the right people is critical. We've had another board meeting. Building rapport with the new investors has been my top priority. I'm also frequenting business associations in town. It's an endless list."

Looking at Watson, he said, "You don't look happy."

"My sense is you've become mired in all the execution aspects of the business. While it's natural to expect it, I see the danger of you overlooking the other strategic elements."

Trent winced.

Watson pressed, "You were excited when we discussed the idea of tracking opportunity quality in the sales pipeline. Is that still a good idea or not? You don't know because it's no longer your focus."

Trent fidgeted. "I see what you're saying. I had finally worked through all the issues related to the management team and the board... I just began to focus on..."

"On things you like to do. I can understand and I appreciate that. However, that's the trap. As CEO, you've got to make sure you pay enough attention to things that don't interest you as much, but are important to Hintec."

Trent was quiet. Then he said, "I did take my eye off the ball and just focused on the tactical aspect of sales, ignoring its strategic aspects. I will refocus to understand if our sales strategy is working and what we need to do to advance it."

"When you're in the office, the cacophony of things can be overwhelming. We need to meet on a regular basis, to talk about your focus and the strategic progress. Our meetings will serve as a reminder to balance strategy with execution."

In the first week of May, Trent handed Watson a sheet of paper as soon as he came through the door. "I received the sales drivers analysis for the first four months of the year.

There's sufficient information here to tell what's working and what isn't. Mitigating risk is the most potent sales driver."

Watson looked at the sheet, listening all the while as the two walked out to the deck. "How have you mitigated the risk for your clients?" he asked.

"We offer them a complete refund of our product fees, if, within six months they decide they don't want it. We do charge them a pro-rated percentage of the support fees, which allows us to cover the cost for our delivery resources."

"And, how's that working?"

"Once our salespeople make this offer, the resistance eases. We've signed several deals."

"Great. What about the other sales drivers, an internal executive champion, and a compelling business event?"

"We've struggled to cultivate champions, but not having them hasn't slowed our pace. We've focused on deals in the $3 million plus range, so we can have at least $500,000 in renewal fees each year. These deals are big to us, but they're small from our client's perspective and don't require an internal executive as a champion. As you know, our clients are multi-billion dollar corporations. When we do deals in the $10 million plus range, we'll need champions."

"And what about compelling business events?"

"The jury is still out. Our salespeople need more training on how to identify and cultivate a compelling event that would cause a prospect to close a deal. Of the three drivers, risk mitigation is delivering for us."

"What else are you doing to mitigate or manage the perception and reality of risk?"

"We have hired industry experts in our four targeted industry sectors. We're going to leverage them to increase our credibility. Also, our most pressing issue last year was client retention. I owe you a lot… client retention has improved by nine percentage points so far this year and the feedback is overwhelmingly positive."

"Which strategic elements has worked for you there?"

"Our client-centric approach. At least half of our upper-tier clients agreed to pay us a higher support fee so we can provide them business-intelligence delivery resources. All of our clients have appreciated our proactive approach. The sales, engineering and value teams have jointly approached clients to review their potential issues, and the management team and I have visited all of our upper-tier clients in the last seven months. All of these steps have changed our client's impression of Hintec."

"Good job."

"And, we're getting ready to work on the third component of our vision, being recognized as a premier BI provider. The first step toward that vision is to generate significant client success stories in our four industry verticals. Those success stories will help us reduce the perception of risk even further."

"What about price and competitive pressures?"

"We've strengthened in both areas. In the past, clients pushed us on price, largely because we hadn't established the value, and were selling to IT management. Now, we take the time to understand the business imperatives. This allows us to sell to executive management. Once we get them to see the value, they're able to do the deals."

"Has your volume of deals picked up?" pressed Watson.

Trent smiled. "I make it sound as if we have many deals under the belt. We're not there yet, but from my detailed questioning of the salespeople, and accompanying many of them on sales calls, I can see the shift in the dialogue with our prospects. Having the business-intelligence delivery resources working closely with the sales team is helping a great deal. We're no longer selling, but instead collaborating with the prospects to solve their needs."

"You're progressing in the right direction."

Trent nodded.

"This transformation is paying dividends. Our customers like it."

"I'm happy for you and for Hintec."

"I keep thinking how you were right in your assessment, and how you kept emphasizing that transformation is continuous. I've had to work hard with Chad and Jeremy, the new leaders of the growth and the value teams. Since neither participated in the process to implement the first cycle, getting them to appreciate the mission, philosophies and vision has been an effort. It helps that they're now part of the second cycle, which is underway."

"As they participate, they'll get to contribute their ideas and develop a sense of ownership," said Watson.

"I sure hope so. Sometimes, I get the sense from Chad, who's an experienced executive that he thinks he might make a better CEO. Normally, I would have been offended and defensive. But, now I take that in my stride. I've sincerely and honestly asked myself if Chad would be a better CEO for Hintec. If he had come eighteen months ago, the answer was a definite yes. But now, Hintec is better served having me as CEO."

"I'm so proud of you. You have looked at the situation from the right perspective. It is the mark of a great servant leader, who thinks of the organization's interest before thinking of his own."

Trent smiled. "Having the senior management team in place is allowing me to extract myself from the daily fire-fighting and focus on the big picture. I'm beginning to think about what we should do differently in the future."

"That's wonderful. That's exactly what I want to hear."

"I'll start thinking about our long-term vision of becoming one of the three largest players in the business-intelligence marketplace, and having at least a third of the market. That's a tall order, and it'll require us to transform again, both internally and externally."

It was the first week in June. Cedric asked Trent to have dinner with him.

After they placed their food order, Cedric said, "I'll be stepping down as chairman at the next board meeting."

"Why?" asked Trent, alarmed.

"That's the agreement I have reached with Jupiter Ventures."

Trent shook his head. "Did they ask to replace me again?"

"No, they're happy with your progress. I'm not sure they see it necessary to have me around. More importantly, they've agreed to buy a majority of my stake in Hintec, thus becoming majority shareholders. For a long time, I've wanted to divest, and step down as chairman."

Trent didn't look happy.

"It makes the most sense for Hintec," comforted Cedric. "Marty Jensen, the CEO of Jupiter Ventures will become chairman. That'll ensure Hintec will be a high priority among their group of portfolio companies."

"I hate to see you go. You've been a guardian angel. Without you, I wouldn't have survived."

"I'll still be available if you ever need me. But I'm sure you'll do just great even otherwise. Let's talk about the other board changes."

After dinner, Trent warmly thanked Cedric again.

The next evening Trent shared his concerns with Watson. "Marty becoming chairman is too much of a spotlight."

"Don't worry. Treat Marty no different than you would've treated Cedric. If your actions are logical and coherent, Marty and Jupiter Ventures will continue to value and respect your leadership."

Later that week, Trent rang Watson's doorbell. "You look excited. Good news?" queried Watson.

"Yes! Wesley Chemicals has re-signed with us," announced Trent as he walked in. "If you remember, I happened onto the CEO in January. It's taken us six months, but we have them back. They signed a $23 million deal. It's our biggest to date!"

"That's wonderful. I'm thrilled for you."

"I couldn't have done it without you. I'm so thankful for all your help. We have a board meeting coming up in July, and I'd like for you to join us at that meeting."

"Why?"

"So you can see the board's reaction to our progress."

"Okay, I'll come. That'll be worth it."

It was July. "We're all set for Catherine's birthday party on Saturday," said Lori as Trent lay on the bed. "Mom is excited about being in Houston for her birthday."

Trent smiled. "I'm glad you are happy. Ever since Catherine was born, things have steadily improved for me."

"Ever since you married me, things have improved for you," said Lori, as she laughed, and poked him in the side.

Watson opened the boardroom door as the board members were seating themselves for their July meeting.

Trent walked over to shake his hand and welcome him. Trent looked at the board members, and said, "Let me introduce to you Mr. Watson Hughes, my advisor, and the real architect behind the success we are experiencing."

Watson nodded in greeting and took a seat.

Cedric started, "We have several important agenda items, but the most important of them all involves Mr. Hughes. Sir, the board of Hintec would be honored if you were to join us as a member of the board."

Watson smiled and turned toward Trent.

"That's right, Mr. Hughes," said Trent. "We would be delighted. As you've often said, transformation needs to be continuous, and having you on the board would be the next level of transformation for Hintec."

Several members nodded encouragement.

Watson looked at the board members and said, "When Trent first suggested I join the board, I was reluctant because I like to see independent board members."

"Me too," jumped in Marty Jensen, the CEO of Jupiter Ventures, and the incoming chairman, "and you couldn't be more independent. Sure, you have acted as Trent's advisor for the last year, but as I understand, you and Trent don't always share the same perspective. And, Trent is convinced you will put Hintec's interests before that of Trent's."

"That I will," said Watson with conviction.

"And that's what makes you a perfect candidate for the board," offered Trent. "Your experience, perspective, and method are invaluable to Hintec. And, as I have shared with Marty, Cedric and the other board members, you will not hesitate to question me or the other management members if we make a mistake. Question not in a critical, but a constructive, respectful and yet incisive manner."

Watson nodded.

Trent continued, "You continue to advise me and urge me to continue to progress on my path of transformation. You have indeed transformed both me and Hintec!"

When Trent finished, Watson said, "I will be happy to serve on the board of Hintec."

The entire board applauded.

"Let me also take this opportunity," said Marty as the applause died down, "to reaffirm our confidence in Trent as CEO. Trent has gone through a steep learning curve and has indeed transformed himself and Hintec. Regardless of how good a method is, the challenge is in implementing it. Watson is the coach, but Trent, you are the quarterback."

Trent smiled. So did Watson.

Marty continued, "We expect you to take on new challenges and generate even more success. We want Hintec to be a shining example to the other companies in our portfolio."

Marty got up and walked over to shake Trent's hand. So did Cedric, Watson and the other board members.

About the Author

Ravi Gopaldas Kathuria

What should a CEO do to lead an organization effectively? Kathuria has been interested in the answer to this question from the early days of his career.

An expert in business performance and organizational dynamics, Kathuria is the founder and president of Cohegic Corporation, a management consulting, executive coaching and sales coaching firm.

Having worked with hundreds of executives, and having led major cross-functional change management initiatives, Kathuria has mastered how to help organizations improve their strategic and execution capabilities.

Kathuria is a vivacious public speaker. Under his leadership, the Houston Planning and Strategic Forum, a non-profit, volunteer organization, grew from a boutique group to Houston's preeminent business association featuring the who's who of major CEOs in Houston.

Kathuria has been a resident of Houston, Texas, for twenty years, before which he grew up in Mumbai, India. He has been married eighteen years to his lovely wife, Seema, and they have two sons, Amrit and Aayush.